DR. DONNA LIGDA

BORN
TO
SELL

· A SALES PRIMER ·

EVERYBODY SELLS

LEARN TO SELL ANYTHING,
TO ANYONE, ANYWHERE.

Letter From Author

Everyone on this planet is both a buyer and a seller at one time or another. If you have what I want and you agree to sell it to me after we mutually agree to price and terms then the deal is done. Both parties come away satisfied with the outcome. This is a straight forward and simple enough concept. Why then is selling for a living such a challenge? And, how does marketing fit into the picture?

In over two decades of training, hiring, leading and managing sales forces on a national scale, I ran into this question as the number one stumbling block to a successful career in sales. As a result, I developed this Sales Primer stripped down to the key components of the sales process. Each word had to count in this succinct approach. As I trained and interacted with more and more potential sales persons, I zeroed in on common themes. Like any solid and stable structure a solid foundation is the number one requirement. That is why we all can relate to the tale of the *Three Little Pigs and the Big Bad Wolf.*

Whether you are considering sales as a career option or already are involved in sales as your profession, this primer is for you. Happy selling!

Credits

I wish to thank Breck and Sharon Ellis for assisting in putting together the site questionnaire. Their experience as a military family who relocated frequently across the globe make them uniquely qualified to light the way for us all.

Web site

I would love to hear from you. Visit me at

www.dr-donna.com and leave a message on my blog

BOOK ONE

BORN TO SELL: A SALES PRIMER

ENDORSEMENTS

DR. DONNA LIGDA

Dr. Ligda provides clarity to the power of selling with practical and proven approaches. Anyone who reads this book can apply this knowledge and these skills to their lives for immediate results.

William Tella
President and CEO
PersonaDX, Inc.

This book debunks the stereotypical view of sales people as backslapping jokesters and emphasizes the reality that the best sales people are well organized professionals. A very important message that needs to be learned in the rapidly changing, global economy if we are to maintain our competitive edge.

Walt Ellis,
Global Recruiter and former global sales manager for two companies

This book is an indispensable dissection of practical sales execution from personal to global relationships. It gives a pervasive first priority to the sales process as used at all levels of exchange: personal, business, organizational, governmental and global.

Charlotte Brechner
27 years as director of sales and owner of a private firm

Ronald Brechner
20 years as sales manager for a multi-million dollar global oil company

Great insight into the world of selling products, services or ideas, a powerful tool to approach the health care market place.

Bonnie Suter,
Hospice Nurse

This book will guide you out of the parochial approach to sales and start your journey into a broader outlook with the objective of being successful in the fast developing global environment.

James Ellis
Former Major, US Army National Guard
Retired Regional Manager, US Customs Service

Whether selling products, services, concepts or ideas, this book offers a strategic roadmap anyone can use. As a healthcare professional in an administrative role, I am always on the lookout for new ways to present ideas that people can "buy into". Dr. Ligda has presented a fresh approach to an age old issue.

Robin Ledyard, MD, MPH
Medical Director of Community Health Benefit
Indianapolis, IN

Born To Sell is an exciting, accessible introduction to one of the most useful selling toolkits for the 21st century. Filled with lively examples from various industries and real people from real companies, the book reveals the power of how selling is the key to most of our successes.

Christy Cirino,
President, Date Intelligence, LLC

From such a complex mind comes the easiest, most flowing and informative book on the subject of sales.

Ron Goldsby
Regional manager of Environmental Services

Dr. Ligda writes, "To sell is to galvanize a relationship." This is a perceptive concept in the development of leaders and mentors as the art of selling is the very foundation for establishing effective communication.

Christine M. Kenar, MA, MT(ASCP) DLM

Dr. Ligda brings a unifying, uplifting theory to sales, self and reality.

John Louis,
National Vice President of Sales

This book provides real options to look at selling in light of shifting world economy.

Ferial Hassan
Human Resources/Administration
South Africa and Florida

OVERVIEW

"The secret of getting ahead is getting started."

—Sally Berger

CHAPTER ONE

Everybody sells. Companies manufacture products that we need, farmers grow our food, doctors provide medical interventions, pharmacies provide drugs designed to treat our ailments, social workers coordinate services in times of stress and need, teachers teach our children, and the clergy provides spiritual direction to guide us in living our lives to the fullest. Examples of how sales activities permeate our everyday lives can go on and on. Wives might convince their husbands of the need for a new home appliance and husbands might convince their wives that those new golf clubs will improve his golf scores or vice-a-versa. The myriad of examples is endless and these types of interactions occur daily across the globe. Whether you are selling a product, an idea, a concept, or a service, the principles remain the same. Sales efforts can be large or small, personal in nature or business related. Whatever the case, everybody sells!

To sell is to galvanize a relationship. Selling is fun, juicy, creative, and is often financially as well as personally rewarding. Sales transactions create a fundamental connection between both parties regardless of who they are or what is being sold. After many years as a player in the game of life I have come to believe that sales make up the "true heart" of not only what we term business transactions but how we interact with everyone we come into contact with in a broader context and on a more personal level. To me, sales are the engine driving the bus, and, therefore, represents a key element of any successful enterprise be it product, idea, concept or service driven.

If you had asked me a few decades ago when I first started my career as a professional health care provider if sales were part of my job description, I probably would have either given you a "deer in the headlights" look or laughed out loud. At that particular phase of my life and career I viewed sales by its most narrow definition of selling goods. One sold products such as soft drinks or cars or clothes. Period.

As I matured and grew in my career, I added services to the rapidly expanding roster of what encompasses sales. I came to understand the link between products and services. My next insight came about when I could separate, explain, understand, and define marketing as a separate function with its own distinct role, outcomes, creativity, and rules. Sales and marketing are two distinct functions both of which are critical to survival in the ever changing landscape of business and life.

Now I am in the twilight of my career and have filled many roles ranging from dog kennel cleaner as a teenager to President of a very successful for-profit company, Board of Director Member and Chairperson of the Board Advisory Committee. Thanks to these experiences, I now comprehend that one literally encounters crap, so to speak, no matter which end of the spectrum he or she is addressing. We have to understand that everything we dream is truly possible and then fulfill that dream with joy and dignity. The challenge is alive and well whether one sells products, services, ideas, or concepts. In actuality, it is often easier to sell tangible products than to sell esoteric ideas and concepts. What is in your field of vision? Let's take a look.

What I particularly enjoy is that involvement in sales is like being inside a living, breathing, talking rainbow because of the diversity of people and their numerous hues and colors. This diversity is accentuated by the places and events that I have participated in and enjoyed. What I have come to appreciate from my interactions with a multiplicity of people from all rungs of life is that basically all of us are connected at the level of spirit regardless of our outer appearances or circumstances. This connection provides us with a common place to start the sales process.

Sales Process

Many of us do not see ourselves as salespeople. We are nurses, doctors, clerks, farm workers, teachers, shop owners, government workers, and so forth. We believe that sales involve the making, selling, and distribution of goods. In actuality, the net of sales is more widely cast encompassing the social sector that provides basic services, the government that provides core laws, armies that protect us, and police that maintain law and order. Each of these unique groups also uses the more traditional goods that are produced.

Skilled salespeople are some of a company's best problem-solvers due to their interaction with the end user of the products and services being provided. They can provide instant feedback from the field perspective to suppliers, manufacturers, engineers, and front office executives. Their movement through a customer's system of handling your products is not static. Their knowledge can and does have a direct impact on the company's bottom line profitability. For instance, my sister heads the IT Department for a fortune 50 company that manufactures and sells heavy earth moving equipment. She is in constant contact with sales to answer questions and determine their needs. My son works for the Denver School System as a Project Manager/IT Consultant and regularly interfaces with teachers and school administration. In the specialty drug market, the field staff provides constant and valuable information on reimbursement problems for very expensive drugs and services. The examples are endless and cover most all industries and service organizations.

Many of us hold a stereotypical vision of top sales people as entertaining, overly friendly, jokesters who are generally male. In reality, the best sales people come in both genders, are well prepared and organized, are professional in the way they conduct themselves, have excellent follow through skills, are well versed and knowledgeable about their products or services, are true problem solvers, and listen more than they talk. They are smart and tenacious in their approach to problem solving.

People with extraverted personalities tend to exude more personal charisma and therefore have a slight edge in interacting with others. However, since all behavior is learned, anyone can increase his or her likeability factor. If you lean towards being more introspective, you will need to ratchet up your presentation abilities, focus on how others perceive your personality, and practice being more open and engaging. If you already possess a sparkling personality keep in mind that charisma always has to be backed up by true skill otherwise it can be viewed as a ruse.

The sales role has both individual entrepreneurship and team focused goals built into it. The sales process allows the salesperson to compete against him or herself. But sales is also a team sport. Team building and cooperation to reach common goals create an environment where people can share ideas.

Work groups can be formed to address and solve mutual problems, and since sales encompasses all aspects of a business, this spirit of cooperation will lead to bigger and better profits. Everyone up and down the company hierarchy will embrace and approve of this outcome.

However, this spirit of cooperation can be tough for some sales people to embrace. When this is the case, it is critical for the sales leader to step in and channel this sales team member in the right direction. Slackers can also pull the team down. Failure to proactively address these destructive behaviors often has disastrous results on the morale of all concerned parties and has led to many such individuals being invited to find new employment opportunities elsewhere.

In the for-profit world, most salespeople are risk takers and value money as a reward. Their personalities allow them to be high risk takers who enjoy and expect high rewards for their achievements. A good and successful sales person is worth every penny of their compensation package. It is a "quid-pro-quo" because if the sales person correctly does the job of selling then the business's bottom line also benefits.

In the case of not-for-profits, the positive operating margin generated provides the funds for reinvestment. At one Catholic non-profit facility I worked with early in my career the nuns used to say, "No margin, no mission." That group of nuns has only grown and prospered through the years while many other orders in the same locale have folded their tents and slipped silently away. Thus one of my early career truths is that all companies, regardless of how they are structured, must have a positive bottom line to survive and thrive. This truth had a profound impact on my subsequent decision making throughout my long career.

The former British Prime Minister, Tony Blair, told Yale's graduating class of 2008 that partnerships are the key to avoiding conflict in an emerging global economy. He cited China and India as two countries with enormous populations that are becoming more powerful. It was noted that for the first time in several centuries' power is moving towards the East. Following World War Two the United States made up 60% of the world's economy. That percentage has dropped to 25%

today. Blair predicted that China and India will industrialize at a rate five times faster than the United States. While it is predicted that the United States will not enjoy this type and rate of growth in the future, our knowledge, management skills, computer expertise, education levels, and vast industrial infrastructure will play a significant role in the emerging world.

Education gives us wings to soar to new heights, but sales provide us with the necessary or desired goods for the journey, including the supplies used in education everywhere. On a sponsored trip to visit the many wonders of Egypt and its amazing culture and history, the tour guide suggested we take boxes of pencils to give to the children as wood is scarce in Egypt. This suggestion turned out to be well received demonstrating that even simple goods allow us to live our lives to the fullest in the manner we choose for ourselves and our families. It is no great mystery that developing countries demand a greater quantity of goods and services for their emergence into the world economic markets. Goods and services provide options. Enlightenment raises awareness, enriches opportunity, and provides lifestyle alternatives, knowledge, and leads to personal empowerment. New skills lead to greater independence, freedoms, insight, and strength. Thus the new emerging market can find its wings and soar.

What is true of sales is also true of most professions, and this is both the best of times and the worst of times to be in sales. The world as we know it is dramatically shrinking, time is speeding up, new knowledge is coming at us at the speed of a run-a-way train, social conventions are dramatically being altered, and new players are flooding the world markets. It is now estimated by some scholars that we have a complete new set of knowledge every three months! This flood of information creates issues relating to quality, language and custom challenges, an uneven playing field in many markets, and a tremendous void of talent to lead the charge. Throw in wide spread corruption in some key markets, and therein lies a mind-blogging challenge along with tremendous opportunities.

As the globe shrinks our need for new knowledge grows and intensifies. In order to successfully build a business platform, several tools and skills must be honed to a sharp, well-defined edge. Time must be carved out of already packed schedules to learn about the opportunities being developed. To use the triple excuses of no time, no money and no energy will only lead to potential failure and missed opportunities.

Sales savvy is critical to success in this growing, paradigm-shifting environment. It's a new, smaller world we find ourselves living and playing in. Seizing the multitude of opportunities created by this paradigm shift in the emerging world marketplace will require skill, tenacity, knowledge, risk taking, intuition, and the ability to read the market correctly. Are you ready to play? Are you hungering for the past or do you find yourself thirsting for the future? The answer is simple. The future is yours to create and you have control over the outcome. No one else can do it for you nor would you want them to do so. Be brave enough to not allow any opportunity to pass you by on your march toward success.

REMARKS

Dr. Donna Lidga

KEY POINTS FROM CHAPTER ONE

1. Every person is involved in the sales process at its most fundamental core. Broadly stated, sales involve the exchange of goods, services, life skills and functions to benefit others.

2. The production of goods and services for sales is shifting to the emerging economies in the East such as India and China.

3. Development time for emerging nations to bring goods and services to market is five to six times faster due to a host of new technology and communication tools. The resultant opportunities are fast paced.

4. Regardless of outer appearance or circumstances, all people are connected at the level of spirit. This fundamental connection can aid in the establishment a sales process.

5. A topnotch salesperson knows and can demonstrate to others how to use his or her products.

6. A sales staff provides invaluable feedback and market intelligence to his or her company leaders, engineers, accounting department, billers, shippers, packers, etc. as to how services and products are being received and used.

7. Sales is a team sport!

8. People attracted to sales like money. A true salesperson will work hard to be a top earner and deserve every penny of their compensation package.

9. Corruption in some world markets will hamper the sales process. Enter at your own risk or not at all.

10. Time is speeding up. The world as we know it is shrinking and old paradigms are fading away. Chaos always creates new opportunities. Be ready!

REMARKS

Dr. Donna Lidga

"The time is always right to do what is right."
—Dr. Martin Luther King, Jr.

CHAPTER TWO
How to Visualize Success

Like all personal endeavors and achievements in our lives, the motivation, skills and abilities to excel in a sales role must come from within each person. Many people seemingly slide through their lives not fully grasping this key, fundamental truth and they are rarely successful or happy. There is no one alive today, no one who has ever lived in the past, and probably no one to be born in the future capable of dwelling inside our brains and thinking for us. If the job is to get done, it's up to you!

Success can be defined in many ways and each of us is different in the route we take to achieve success. While the methods may vary, there are basic tenants and personal attributes that help you in achieving your personal sales goals. They are self-awareness, commitment, caring, self-confidence, product knowledge, product commitment, belief in one's self, self awareness, communication skills, and a desire for success. You have to want to succeed. What lurks beneath the surface of our minds can sink our efforts and lead us to the vortex of defeat if we don't make the effort or take the time to address these demons with candor and resolve.

Self Awareness

The first step is always the most difficult and requires the greatest honesty along with accurate and probing introspection into what one truly believes and wants to achieve with their life. We must define what success means to each of us and be absolutely clear in our minds what we want to achieve. This is not the place for censorship. Get rid of the inner voice saying, "I shouldn't feel this way" or "so and so won't approve. This is your process and your livelihood. What do you want to achieve?

I went into sales because I like money. I don't worship money but I do find money to be a useful tool in day-to-day living. I've been both dirt poor, resorting to collecting glass bottles alongside the road to redeem for the deposit money to buy milk and bread, and I've also been very successful in my life. I much prefer being successful and, in truth, I have been able to help many more people including my family, by enjoying a state of affluence as opposed to a state of poverty. So can you.

Commitment and Caring

Many times we fail because we aren't fully committed to achieving our goals. Commitment requires that we display the self-discipline and caring to stay focused on the end goal of making the sale or providing the services.

Commitment means hauling your butt out of bed when an extra hour of sleep sounds so enticing. Time and energy are required to get the job done correctly.

This is not the time to sugar coat the facts and take shortcuts. Procrastination leads to someone else being invited to eat your lunch. Stay focused and on-point. Individual behaviors are important, are regularly viewed by others, and often reflect poorly on your organization. If severe enough they can also lead to you being escorted out the door. Do what is right, not what is easy.

Your customers or clients know when you are sincere, honest, caring and enthusiastic. Ask any parent to identify how important it is to hold onto core values when instructing children in making life decisions. Your success will come through many people in your career. You will find that others tend to help those individuals whom they can relate to especially if they believe that the salesperson can help solve a service problem that requires fixing. You want all your customers to tell others: "I give him/her all my business because they take care of my small problems before they become large problems. They support me."

This is true whether you are selling a product of providing a service. Stick by your customer through good economic times and lean times. All of us appreciate a physician or nurse practitioner who spends time with us talking and teaching us how to achieve greater health. The same is true for our pastor, investment counselor, banker, grocer, mechanic, or anyone else providing a service to help us live our lives more fully and safely.

Self-Confidence

Self-confidence is another one of those "inside traits" that gets projected into the outside world for all to experience. Unfortunately, we can't put on a happy face and fake it until we make it with this one. Authenticity matters. When confidence is absent, it creates a noticeable void. Over time a lack of self-confidence causes stagnation and often leads to a failure to advance.

What is required is a belief in yourself. Believe that you can accomplish your goals. Block all thoughts of failure out of your mind and only concentrate on the desired outcome. If you experience a misstep, learn from it and get right back on the sales target. Recognize that failure is part and parcel of the sales process, just as it is in life in general. Learn from your mistakes and continue striving toward your sales target. There is a cosmic law that states that we grow into what we believe ourselves to be. Be the best, the most successful salesperson in your company. Make it true with confidence. This outcome can only be achieved in the physical, everyday world by first believing it deep within one's self. Belief in one's self and one's abilities is an inside job. No one else can do it for you. By the same token no one can take it away from you either. It belongs to you and only you.

Enthusiasm

After love, which is the most powerful of all emotions in the universe, enthusiasm is the single most contagious emotion. People really get charged about individuals who express their excitement about what they are doing. It's something that you can't fake. In the emotional roller coaster of sales, it is tough to remain perpetually positive. However, in front of customers, it is an absolute necessity. If you are having that terrible day where you just cannot manufacture a positive attitude, go home and do paperwork! Your customers do not want to see a grump. If you are having more down days than fun days, go back to step one. Ask yourself if sales are really what you want to do as your career choice.

There are situations that may preclude you from withdrawing from the sales call as an option regardless of how you are personally feelings or what life challenge you may be personally experiencing. There are techniques that can be successfully applied in these types of situations and specific techniques that can be used will be addressed in later chapters.

Beliefs

Successful sales are built on emotion. Successful results in sales begin and end with your brain. Along the way success also touches the heart and the hands. The brain allows us to dream our goals, the heart allows us to believe we can achieve our goals, and the hands allow us to live our dream of realizing our goals. Our success always comes in two parts: our personal achievements and then sharing with others what we are attempting to achieve. A large part of any salesperson's success comes from communicating thoroughly and frequently with the support team at the home office. Accounting, shipping and receiving, finance, operations, manufacturing, engineering, customer support, and other elements all must be kept in the loop to successfully complete the sales process.

There is nothing more frustrating to the sales person than to have the sales process botched up by the home office. Some of the most heated, tension filled corporate confrontations that I have ever witnessed in my career have occurred between field salespeople and corporate support employees. These range from shipping errors, delays in delivery dates, incorrect order fills, and billing errors just to name a few common examples. This level of confrontation is a "no win" scenario and often requires the support of sales management to be successfully resolved.

Whenever possible, the field sales staff should be encouraged to spend time with the corporate support team to get to know them personally and to give the support staff a firsthand account of why it is so important to meet the customer's expectations. This is no less true for anyone providing a service. Reliance on the whole team doing their portion of the job at hand is paramount to success for all involved.

Sales Success

Sales success begins with perception. Our only limitation to gaining success is an inability to use our imagination to see that success fully realized. Set your goals and focus on the desired outcome. Believe in yourself. Trust the process. Fear and doubt are your greatest enemies. Fear and doubt rob us of our purpose and goals by derailing our focus. We can get so caught up in a "woe is me" mentality that we create a circle of fear and just keep looping endlessly around, never moving forward. Don't give in to these twin demons and let them dictate your life. It will be easy to tell what is happening in your life because advancement versus remaining stuck are not parallel tracks. If you are not moving forward, you are stuck. Do whatever is necessary to break this pattern.

KEY POINTS FROM CHAPTER TWO

1. All the key attributes of a successful sales person comes from within their own thought patterns. There is only one person occupying your brain's thought process and that is you.

2. Visualization of a successful outcome in your sales process is a powerful tool. Use it!

3. Self-awareness requires us to be brutally honest in self-evaluating our talents and skills. What do you really want to achieve?

4. Product knowledge is a key element of any type of sale. Become the company's expert.

5. If you are not 100% committed to your product or service, someone else who is, will eat your lunch and you will be shown the door.

6. Offer true help to your customers and they will respond to you when you need them. Selling is a "give and take" process.

7. Enthusiasm is a contagious emotion. No one enjoys working with a grump. If you must, fake it until you make it.

8. Believe in yourself. Believe you can achieve your goals. Learn from your mistakes, don't dwell on them, and move on. View your mistakes as your greatest teacher in life and in

the work setting.

9. Success comes in two forms: personal achievements and sharing those achievements with others. Sharing builds trust and confidence.

10. Sales success begins with envisioning a successful outcome. Happy selling!

Dr. Donna Lidga

"If you think you can or you think you cannot, either way you are right."

—Henry Ford

CHAPTER THREE
Competition

It's everywhere! There is no escaping competition. Learn to deal with it. Your success or your failure depends on how well you master the realities of the market.

The world is shrinking and competition is red hot. Sales methodologies are changing fast, and the internet has brought the world together like no other medium throughout history. The internet has opened the pathway for individualized players and small to medium companies to compete against the large, well established industrial giants.

Emerging economies now have the means to truncate their development curve, leap-frog over years of building infrastructure, and emerge a hungry, roaring beast wanting to be fed their share of the market products. This fact is creating opportunities that never existed before. It is also creating a strain on natural resources and a new way of doing business wherein no one has the edge of full knowledge. Like all new market change, this vacuum creates both enormous opportunity and a significant risk of failure.

One key strategy that all successful companies use when facing rapid change is innovation. When the market is in the midst of rapid or radical change and suffering from growing pains the companies that survive and thrive are the ones that innovate. They pay attention to market trends, talk to and analyze what experts have to share, and get their network of customers, salespeople, and industry contacts to weigh in.

In stressful economic times it is so easy to slip into the survival mode and become fixated on slashing costs, squeezing out every ounce of productivity, and looking only at fixing the short-term immediate problem. Survival seems to take up your entire focus and all your time. Yet business also has a longer-term goal and that is to weather the storm, increase sales, and remain profitable in the future. Sales team members can play a key role in indentifying those areas that can contribute to a longer term vision. The company deserves 20 to 25% of its leadership talent, sales time and energy, budget allocation, and infrastructure development devoted to securing its future. The natural human response to all this market stress is to avoid additional conflict. As humans we can easily drown in the fury of the storm.

One of my all time favorite cartoons hung on the wall of the purchasing agent in an organization where I worked for over a dozen years. It showed an old fashioned Walled City under siege. The ground troops and the defending Walled City troops were all shooting at each other with bows and arrows. The salesperson was standing on the Walled City rooftop offering the purchasing agent a Gatling-gun that could rapidly fire off a bullet per second. The caption under the cartoon read: "Not now. Can't you see that I am busy?" How often do we get caught up in the crisis of the moment and miss the opportunity to implement real and lasting change and innovation. The opportunities for innovation are there. Take the time to identify them. Change agents are rare. Significant change requires a person who is willing to stick his or her neck on the chopping block in order to achieve the future that they envision. Change requires the ability to perceive what lies around the corner where no one has a clear line of vision. Change agents often have to be willing to put their careers on the line, take a personal risk, and excite other team members to follow. Motivation to be an agent for change comes from many sources, value systems, and beliefs. Often it is no more complex than a truly bored individual desiring the challenge of a new opportunity or change in the status quo.

Sales staff can play an immensely valuable role in this process as they are the feet on the street, the on-site eyes of the company, and they have an ear to the heartbeat of their customers. Often it is the savvy salesperson who first alerts the home office of the impending tsunami.

Sales Role

This emergence in the new world market will increase the salesperson's responsibilities, or, at minimum be a strong influencer, regarding how business is conducted in your industry. Sales representation within a company involves several functions including:

- Managing sales territories
- Defining the sales role and image
- Educating

- Analyzing market trends
- Knowing products well

Managing Sales Territories

The definition of territory is nothing more than the geographical boundaries of your area of promotion and a list of all the existing and potential customers within that area. Territory management begins by identifying all potential customers in that geographic space. The process is the same for service providers who must identify their service area. Once all the existing and potential new customers have been identified, a call list is developed. This is a basic and straight forward process.

Although the process is basic and straight forward, it is the bane of many a salesperson who receives more "no's than yeses". A person's feelings of self-worth can be assaulted by toxic levels of rejection. It is therefore imperative that the process of prospecting be understood and its associated negativity guarded against. View these calls as an opportunity to hone and refine your sales techniques and skills. Results will follow.

Exploratory sales calls are the perfect opportunity to refine your bag of sales tools and supplies. First you need dependable, reliable transportation. You should never be late for a sales call if you can possibility avoid it. Fill your toolbox with business cards, a variety of marketing materials, thank-you notes, follow-up appointment cards, a laptop computer, a well-rehearsed 30 to 45 second elevator speech, a list of goals achieved, and basic office supplies such as a stapler, sticky notes, pencils and pens.

A map of the territory. Mark your current customers and their sales volumes. Include all the available targets within the territory with their potential sales volumes along with as much known information as you can glean. The size of the territory is immaterial as the process is the same. Example: In specialty pharmacy, certain orphan disease states (which are rare and expensive to treat) require that children be monitored by a medical specialist. These families tend to cluster in about a two hour driving radius around large teaching hospitals giving them ready access to the specialists who have the ability to treat their child.

Winning begins and ends with your belief system. Henry Ford said it best. If you think you can, you are right. If you think you can't, you are right. Belief in your self is the greatest predicator of success.

There is a proverb from the Song of Solomon in the Old Testament about how birds of the field neither toil nor sow, yet they are arrayed more splendidly than King Solomon, one of the richest kings ever to have lived. Yet, God did not throw food into the bird's nest. The bird still has to go seek food for themselves. It is the same with sales. Opportunities are out there. You just have to seek them out.

Definition of Sales Role and Image

You are in the spotlight when you sell. Selling is high-profile. You become the embodiment of your company and its values and show them off to everyone with whom you meet and interact. Your company will be judged by your behavior, manner of dress, how well informed you are about your products and services, your social skills (or lack thereof) and your actions. When living in a fish bowl, it pays to keep the water clean and clear.

Time and distance become irrelevant to sloppy social behavior. At one time I was living on the east side of Florida and my salesperson lived in southern California over 3000 miles away. When she became loud and disruptive at an educational event due to excessive alcohol intake among a large gathering of potential families and clients, I knew about it once she was being hauled into a safe driver car to be taken home. My point is that we live in a shrinking world and have the ability to instantly communicate over any distance, great or small. Cameras on cell phones often capture our behavior, which is what occurred in this incident. Fortunately for all concerned, rehabilitation medical treatment was offered by the company and accepted by the employee.

Whenever penetrating a new market never ignore the rules of social engagement. Always do your homework! Know what to wear to dinner, what gifts or flowers are acceptable, who is expected to pay the bill, how liquor is handled, roles of men and women, topics to discuss during dinner, and topics to avoid. Once I brought flowers to a client that are exclusively reserved for funerals in that particular culture! This small act created a great deal of laughter at my expense, and while no lasting damage was done, I never, ever made that mistake again.

The topics of customs, social interaction, and social conventions are detailed more extensively in chapter ten.

Be an Educator

One of the primary functions of any sales person is education. Salespeople must be adept at presenting the key aspects of their organization or company along with its products and services. It is an unforgiveable sin to not know who you work for in terms of what products and services they provide. In very large, technical and geographically dispersed organizations, it is acceptable to know how to get the information and then follow up and make the appropriate connections.

The single trait that will separate you from your competitors is your knowledge base. Become the source of information, the "go to" person, so that your clients come to rely on you as a source of information for referrals and product knowledge. Show each company that you actively engage with how to manage and expand their business more effectively. The more these organizations grow, the more your sales increase.

Market Trend Analysis

The growth of your company is contingent upon the company's ability to respond to change and emerging market trends. You are the "feet-on-the-street" so you are in the best position to provide valuable information and key insights into your company's leadership team. You can evaluate competitors' efforts, listen and identify emerging trends and changes, and generate new marketing ideas, new programs and services, along with key pricing strategies. Market intelligence is essential for the salesperson. You are in a unique position to feed information to the home office. Be alert to sudden competitor activity in new acquisitions, joint ventures, and any other changes in the way competitors approach the market. A word of caution here, information and market intelligence is powerful and valuable. Don't give yours away and don't cross any legal lines in gaining information. The fallout can be and most often is lethal to your career, if not your wallet or your freedom.

You are unique. There is no one exactly like you. Your sales style should fit and compliment your personality. Never try to be something you are not. It's guaranteed that this approach will make you come across as a phony. Approach the role of sales with a positive attitude. The bottom line is simple. People buy from people they like and respect. How many people do you like and respect that are constantly negative, have a "gloom and doom" approach to life, or who are constantly cynical? Enthusiasm is contagious. If you are genuinely excited about what you do, your customer will be also. Real sales leadership requires that you can get in touch with others. Know their needs, wants, desires, and problems and connect with them on human level.

RULE: Never, ever say anything negative about the competition. This is a cardinal rule in sales and it is not worth the negative fallout that indulging yourself in snake pit behavior will create. Your job is to present yourself and your company in the best, most constructive manner possible. Take the high road even inside your own organization.

Once upon a time in the distant past of my career, a co-worker of mine took it upon himself to constantly notify our CEO of what he perceived to be all my management deficiencies. I out ranked him in the organization as I was Chief Operating Officer and he was Vice President. One Christmas, this VP took it upon himself to call the CEO during the CEO's well deserved vacation to once again lodge a complaint about me. His complaint was regarding a relatively minor business issue that I had already resolved. I had also sent the CEO a brief report on the problem and my resolution. The CEO's reaction was swift and lethal. The Vice President was fired and he received no sympathy from anyone, including me. No one wins the game of one-upmanship. Your job is to sell your company and its products or services. Give negative behavior a pass.

Product Knowledge

In today's rapidly changing, competitive marketplace, it is imperative that you understand every aspect of your customer's needs and every detail about your products or services. You want to seal your relationship with your customers by providing them accurate information and becoming their "go-to" expert. This will keep your business relationships sealed, your wallet full, and you can bank on being part of the team. You have made yourself part of the solution by resolving your customer's problems.

We often hear the phrase, "the customer is always right." While this attitude is correct, the statement is not necessarily true. Your customer may be legitimately confused and it is up to you to clear up the confusion. This action can be tricky and often requires great tact and diplomacy on your part so as not to offend. Always strive to talk with your customer in private when an issue like this arises. No one likes to be called to task in a public forum and especially not in front of subordinates. It is humiliating and unnecessary.

Conclusion

Sales success begins by perceiving a successful outcome. Your only limitation in gaining success is the extent of your ability to use your imagination to see your success fully realized. As with any vision for success, the steps are simple: dream the end goal, believe in yourself and your abilities, and live every moment. It is the second step that causes most of us problems. It's the step where doubts and fears enter the picture. Remain positive no matter what is lurking around you and you will succeed. Avoid playing the "ain't it awful" game as negativity only leads to a dead end.

Selling is interesting in the realm of human behavior in that we don't like to be solicited, but we love to buy. Selling involves a great deal of emotional investment. The hook is to identify the buyer's needs and wants. The more you are in tune with what the buyer is actually seeking, the greater, your sales numbers will be. The internet is an immensely valuable tool that has made it much easier to obtain data on your potential customers. By the same token, there can be so much data available that sensory overload frequently occurs. Learn to quickly separate the wheat from the shaft.

In the not-for-profit world, data overload is often the case. Data is needed to be used for its intended purpose of finding information that leads towards solid outcomes and sound decision making. Data can also be misused to blur facts, tilt outcomes in a desired direction, obscure underlying economic factors, and obscure direct public sentiments by preying on personal fear factors. It pays to stay informed, ferret out the facts, and act responsibility.

KEY POINTS FROM CHAPTER THREE

1. Competition is a given in the sales role. Your success or failure in sales depends on how well you master the realities of the market, which is in an enormous state of flux.

2. The internet has shrunk the world, opened new pathways for conducting business, and placed the world markets in warp-speed intensity. Like all new far-flung market changes, the internet has created both enormous opportunity and significant risk.

3. One key strategy to meet rapidly changing market conditions is innovation. Listen to sales staff out in the field. They are usually the first ones to identify the impending tsunami.

4. Use a written plan of action to manage your territory. A person's sense of self-worth can be assaulted by toxic levels of rejection. Being prepared with a full tool box gives you confidence. Your initial impression will be made the first two seconds of meeting a potential client. Make those seconds count!

5. Selling is high profile. You become the embodiment of your company. When living in a fish bowl, it pays to keep the water sparkling clear and clean.

6. Product education is one of the salesperson's primary responsibilities. It is an unforgiveable

sin to not have a complete working knowledge of what you are selling. Failure to master product knowledge rapidly leads to "death" in your role as a salesperson.

7. Salespeople are the "feet on the street," providing valuable information and insights regarding market conditions.

8. Never, ever say anything negative about the competition. This is the cardinal rule in sales. The negative fallout is not worth it. Concentrate your efforts on what makes your products or services superior.

9. Become the "go-to" expert for your customers. This role will seal your relationship and also be very profitable.

10. Learn how to handle awkward situations with your customers in private. Tact and diplomacy win out every time over ridicule and humiliation. Remain positive no matter what is lurking around you and you will succeed.

Dr. Donna Lidga

"The expectations of life depend upon diligence; the apprentice that would perfect his work must first sharpen his tools."
—Confucius

CHAPTER FOUR
Territory Management

Another name for territory management is planning. Planning is the key to sales success even though planning doesn't sound particularly sexy or exciting. In fact, good planning is the key to success in most human endeavors. The rule of thumb is the larger the project, the longer the planning cycle. For example, it took two years of intense planning alone to put the first man on the moon. Many new product launches take 12 to 18 months, and computerization and integration on an international scale can take three to five years to plan and implement successfully.

This is where we dive into the nitty-gritty of sales. There are many tools available to assist you in your sales role. Start with learning all there is to know about your assigned territory. Quality information, solid planning, a schedule of sales calls, follow-up skills, and determination are keys to success. If you don't know where you are going, it doesn't matter how you get there. This step organizes your sales territory by identifying all existing and potential customers.

The planning step is no less important in the non-profit arena. Let's say you want to locate a new site to build a church or open a food pantry. All the steps identified below are germane to the process. The same blocking and tackling is required for success.

Your potential sales list is derived from many sources, including:

- A company's previous territory records
- The phone book
- Current business partners
- The internet
- Professional directories
- City directories

Previous Territory Records

This is a gift to you but you still have the responsibility to verify all the submitted data for accuracy. Many times you will be assigned to open up a virgin territory, therefore no information will be complied. It then becomes your responsibility to put together a detailed territory plan and to map out the potential business locations.

Phone Book

Phone book yellow pages remain a valid, free source of business listings. Since a business may list under several categories, make sure you cross reference so that you don't miss any potential customers.

Current Business Partners

Your current business partners are often more than willing to share valuable information with you. Talk to suppliers, purchasing agents, administrative assistants, warehousing, Vice Presidents of operations, and anyone else who has their hand on the pulse of your industry.

Don't forget to return the favor when asked. This is an excellent way to build your team-player imagine. Play it forward.

Internet

It is sometimes difficult to remember life before the internet. In just a few short years this means of electronic communication has fundamentally altered our way of life and opened up opportunities heretofore never dreamed possible. The amount of information that can be captured is staggering. The internet is a tool that helped elect the first person of color as President of the United States in 2008. Barack Obama makes extensive use of the internet as a communication tool. In popular culture, it allows millions of people to vote for their favorite competing new talent singing star each week on shows like American Idol. It can create overnight stars such as the singer, Susan Boyle, from Scotland. The examples go on and on. Tap into this incredible resource.

Over the past three to five years several new sites of social networking and even business networking have sprung up. Some of the larger, well known sites are Twitter.com, LinkedIn.com, Facebook.com, and Myspace.com. Blackberries, iPhones and iPods are even being used by the Vatican to broadcast the Pope's messages to the world. Networking as a business strategy is not a new concept. But what are new are the computer tools that are now available to us that dramatically increase the speed of communication. Depth of numbers of people targeted and the far flung reach of out networking around the globe is instant. We live in a global world that is just beginning to be developed and explored. The rewards and the risks will attract prospectors much like a gold rush or the discovery of a new oil field.

To date these sites are not meant for direct selling of your products but they are a new marketing tool for the 21st century. Networking sites can be used to inform people of new product launches, new books set to be published, and new services that will be available. They can also showcase staff achievements, accolades received, community services being provided or promoted, and a host of other information. This new marketing approach makes perfect use of the concept that all of us are linked together by only two to seven degrees of separation. This networking linkage is just one more way that we are rapidly becoming a global community. Learn to use these new tools effectively. The time has truly arrived to think outside of old paradigms and explore the vast new global horizons that have merged through technology, speed and lower costs.

Like any new relationship, there is a love-hate component imbedded in managing this potent new technology. Employees could potentially send sensitive company information into cyber space with a click of a button. Once the message is sent, there is no recall button. A personal or business reputation can be severely damaged as a result of this one action. Once the deed is done, recovery can be painfully complex and the damage extensive, therefore expect to see strident policies and severe penalties in the future around the issues of internet misuse and misconduct. Many companies have already developed legal policies on the consequences to employees associated with misuse of company information, sharing of competitive information, or distributing negative or unflattering comments regarding the company or its leadership.

Professional Directories

Most professional groups publish an annual guide of their membership with contact information. These publications are often very expensive. My recommendation is to access the guide through your public library or online if it is published. While expensive, membership mailing lists are also available and can be worthwhile to purchase.

City Directories

Most cities still publish information about local businesses. Generally this publication is free of charge and many smaller businesses and start-ups tend to use this method of advertising. I recently used the services of a young, very talented graphic artist who was using this approach to launch his graphic art business. I was very pleased with the results.

Tips for Organizing Your Territory

Now that you have laid the foundation of all the potential customers in your assigned territory, the second step is to set up a call schedule. Consider these tips as complete this step.

Use a map of your territory to physically identify the location of each potential account.

- Use different colored pins to mark locations on your territory map to denote distance, stratification of accounts by size, differentiation between potential volume of business, existing customers versus potential new customers, or any other coding system that is meaningful to you.

- Use your map to develop a realistic call schedule. This step can be simple in small geographic territories or complex in large geographic territories. In either case, the process remains the same.

Most of us in sales believe that using a circular geographic approach to segmenting your territory is the most time and energy efficient. If possible, make your first call of the day closest to your starting point. At the mid-point of your day, schedule sales calls at the far point of your circle. Complete your day by making your last call nearest to your starting point in your circle. This approach maximizes selling time and minimizes windshield time.

Face to face time is extremely important in the sales process and your goal is to get as much face time as possible. Plan your day out in advance, make appointments whenever possible, be on time, and communicate any unforeseen delays. Let your client know that you recognize that his time is important to you.

The number of calls that can be made per day is highly variable depending on your industry, geographical distance to be covered, amount of personal interaction that is required at every visit, and whether you have a virgin territory that requires development time or a well established territory. Most frequently you can anticipate having a mixed territory of existing accounts and potential new accounts along with a myriad of other factors to consider. Each industry and company sets sales goals. Become very familiar with your company and industry expectations. Sales staffs are usually rewarded through the use of a performance based formula.

Performance based formulas for sales are among the most fair and equitable methods of compensating sales staff with some practical caveats. Beware of any hidden pitfalls in these plans. Common limitations can include caps on earning potential or performance tied directly to how the company performs overall (which you do NOT have direct control over). It pays to read the fine print and negotiate your total compensation package. Top notch sales staff can earn more than anyone else in the company. This fact makes some bureaucrats uncomfortable and brings out their need to place controls on the sales staff.

Establish the best time to visit with each customer or potential customer. Demonstrate that you are respectful of their time schedule.

Don't forget to schedule time for phone calls, paperwork, completing and submitting weekly sales reports, talking with your boss and other co-workers, completing and submitting expense reports, and laying out your next round of sales calls. As the sign posted on the inside of the bathroom toilet door empathically states, the job is not done until the paperwork is complete! In looking over my career in sales, I fired more sales people for chronically being non-compliant with basic office reporting than any other misdeed. This is sad because it is a completely avoidable situation.

If you are adverse to office paperwork seek other methods for being compliant. Enlist your spouse, your computer savvy kids, a per hour administrative assistant, your accountant, or any responsible adult who can handle this task for you. Don't forget to buy them a nice birthday gift in addition to the fees you pay them. Overall, the smartest course of action is to "suck it up" and realize that every job has its tedious aspects. Use the past week to evaluate your results and act as a springboard to lay out your sales plan for the coming week. Consistency is the key to good territory management. Strive for a degree of coverage for every existing account and every potential new account.

KEY POINTS FROM CHAPTER FOUR

1. Territory management is the nitty-gritty of planning. Planning is the key to sales success even though it may not sound particularly sexy or exciting.

2. Many sources exist to assist you in territory planning and new methods are constantly arising. Some of the standards are your company's previous territory records, phone books, current business partners, suppliers and vendors, directories of professional organizations and city directories.

3. A powerful new source of business identification along with contact information is the internet. More and more businesses, both large and small, have websites.

4. Be aware of the emerging trend of internet sites like Twitter.com and LinkedIn.com which is geared toward marketing. While these sites are not intended for the direct selling of products and services, they can be used to spotlight new product launches, showcase new books getting ready to be published, inform readers about staff achievements, and highlight community activity of your company.

5. Use territory maps to identify by location existing clients and potential new business clients. When possible, use a circle to plot your travel each day. Start with sales calls closet to your starting point, move farthest away mid-day, and then move closet to your desired ending point for the last call of the day.

6. Face to face time is extremely important in sales. Your goal is to get as much face time as possible. Let your client know that you appreciate their time. Notify your client of unavoidable delays.

7. Most sales staff members are compensated based on their individual performance. A highly skilled sales person can command a compensation package approaching or exceeding that of his or her boss. Make certain you read the fine print and that you completely understand how your compensation is determined. Don't be derailed by a sloppy understanding of the fine print.

8. Most of us don't enjoy paperwork. We find it boring and mundane even while we recognize its importance. There are many helpers available to you for completing this task such as your husband or wife, kids when they are old enough to be trusted with this level of work, administrative assistants or accountants. The very best approach is to "suck it up" and use this task as a planning tool for creating your next week's schedule.

9. Consistency is the key to good territory management. Strive for coverage in existing accounts along with every potential new account.

10. Quality information, solid planning, a schedule of sales calls, follow-up, delivering what has been promised, and the will to succeed are the keys to success in sales.

Dr. Donna Lidga

"Zeal without knowledge is fire without light."
—Dr. Thomas Fuller

CHAPTER FIVE
Close Encounters of the Productive Kind

We have established the basic but vital preparation required to organize your sales or service territory. Your sales toolbox is now filled with all the key components which you will need to make that first sales call. Shoes are shined and itineraries are printed out with your schedule, maps, and pertinent notes. Whenever possible, appointments have been arranged and you know who to seek out at each location on your schedule by name and position. Emergency contact information is available to use in case of unforeseen delays.

Your 30 second introductory speech has been honed to pure perfection because you realize how little time is available to make a positive first impression on the potential client. People buy from people they like. On average you have two seconds to make a client like you! In that two seconds the human brain takes in how you look both physically and emotionally, whether you are smiling, how organized you appear, the degree of your nervousness, the firmness of your hand shake, your confidence level, how genuine you are, and your likeability quotient. This is the point for inserting your "wow" factor and displaying your humanness. Our ability to make ourselves vulnerable is a strong link that binds humanity together. Make eye contact because this shows your confidence. Avoid the "fiberglass figure" of a painted-on smile, and posed aloof look.

Elicit the help of family members, friends and mirrors for practicing this step until it flows naturally and smoothly. Practice, practice and practice yet again until you have this step nailed down. Practice while considering all sorts of barriers to success. Some common themes that can throw this phase off balance are: interruptions, phone calls, distractions of all kinds, staff wandering into the office, emergencies, time-outs to sign forms, or just plain old fashioned rudeness. The more confident you are, the better your chance of seamlessly picking back up with your presentation. There will also be times when it will be the prudent and the best course of action to reschedule your visit.

Not all of us have an outgoing personality that just naturally sparkles, lighting up everyone around us. Nor are all of us male or female, or tall and willowy. And certainly not all of us look like we're physically related to the ancient gods or popular movie stars. The key is learning to be comfortable and confident in our own skin. Celebrate your particular uniqueness and so will those around you. The task at hand is to sell your goods or services. Stay focused on the goal. People will forget what you said. People will forget what you did. But people will never forget how you made them feel.

I want to share with you a great success story that involves a classmate at the University of Chicago Executive MBA Program. When I attended business school in the late-80s, it was a different world than the one we live in today. There were 66 members in my class and exactly six of us were female. All of us had to have some remarkable credentials to even be admitted to this prestigious program, so my classmates all read like a "who's who" of Chicago business. There were thousands of applicants for these 66 places of honor. Luckily I didn't realize this when I applied or it may have made me a tad uneasy! The point is that we were all already a success in our chosen fields and we were preparing ourselves to be even more successful.

Over the course of two years we learned as much from each other's success and failures as we gleaned from the formal classes. One day the issue of salary came up as it invariably does in these types of settings. I believe that everyone was astonished to learn that one of the females in the class was the highest wage earner. Her story was an inspiration. She informed the class that she learned she was a token hire and that all that truly was expected of her once she was on the payroll was to fill the EEOC quota. As a result, she was stuck in a back office with some obscure financial instruments to play with. No one expected her to be successful in actually selling these instruments.

My classmate felt so insulted by this low expectation scenario that she became motivated to succeed in the face of all odds against her. Applying many of the principals outlined here, she developed a sales plan, worked it diligently, and succeeded beyond anyone's wildest expectations, outstripping everyone else with her annual earnings. So the biggest question to ask yourself is: how badly do you want to succeed? Are you willing to do what it takes to claim success for yourself?

As a reminder, these same principles are applicable to any type of product sales and any sector of services in the not-for-profit arena. Everyone has to identify what services already exist, who the main players are, where opportunities can be had, and all the other details that create your planned targets and approaches.

Proactive Sales Calls

Initial customer calls work best as fact finding missions and several outcomes can be achieved. The objectives related to these calls are as follows:
- Introduce yourself to the client
- Determine your contact person
- Update your records and check them for accuracy
- Gather and record new data

Meticulous recording of pertinent information is critical and is best done while the information remains fresh in your mind. Most of us use laptop computers for storing data, but an accurate and complete paper file can also work well.

Face-to-Face Market Research

The purpose of the initial sales call is to make existing clients aware of who you are. Introduce yourself to the key players and identify what company you represent. Explain who you are, give a short synopsis of your background, define your role within the company, and provide your contact information. Ask if there are any outstanding issues with your company at existing accounts that you can assist in resolving. In a well established territory, it generally works best to call on existing accounts first before tackling potential new customers. This approach provides background in the territory and ensures that any new potential customers will get a positive nod when seeking references from your existing customers.

The purpose of gathering account information is to identify the sales growth from various sources, including:

- Expansion of existing accounts
- New business from existing accounts
- New business from start-up accounts

Gatekeepers

Gatekeepers are a fact of life. Gatekeepers are the people whose task it is to keep outsiders out. Some are strong, some are weak, but all can become your best ally or your worst nightmare. Here are some tips for successfully managing gatekeepers:

- Introduce yourself to the gatekeeper and provide your business card.
- Learn the gatekeeper's name and write it down. Treat the gatekeeper with respect. They have a job to do, too.
- Ask them for pertinent information about how the office handles callers.
- Find out who makes appointments and record their name with correct spelling.
- Find out how many people work in your client's division.

- Ask what kind of token gifts are appreciated and allowed and for how many people. For example, if you want to furnish donuts or company pens, how many should you bring?
- Are flowers allowed at the gatekeeper's desk for all to enjoy?
- Record any other helpful information they can provide.

Build a positive relationship with the guardian of the gate. It pays off.

KEY POINTS FROM CHAPTER FIVE

1. Make your first impression count. Research has shown that you have about two seconds to make a positive first impression. The human mind is faster than any computer and can take in multiple factors simultaneously, including whether you are smiling, your level of confidence, how you are dressed, how friendly you are, how relaxed you appear, and a whole host of data that the person uses to determine whether or not to trust you.

2. People do business with people they like. Nervous, unfriendly, slovenly, or grumpy people don't do well in sales.

3. Prepare yourself for positively dealing with interruptions. Practice until you can pick up your presentation seamlessly. Interruptions are inevitable in a business setting. Learn to deal with interruptions with a smile, even if you have to "fake it" in front of the client.

4. Make the most of your personal assets. Salespeople come in both genders, all age groups, and all sizes and shapes. Celebrate your particular uniqueness and so will those around you. Stay focused on the goal. The task at hand is to sell your goods or services.

5. Meticulous record keeping of your accounts and sales is critical. Record up-to-date information

as quickly as possible. A laptop computer is a valuable tool to use, but an organized paper system also works well. If a salesperson fails at the record keeping step, their departure from the company will soon follow.

6. Fact finding missions have four main goals: introduce yourself, identify the organization's contact person, update existing records with verified accuracy, and gather and record new data.

7. Identify new sources of sales growth from expansion of existing accounts, adding on new business lines to existing accounts, and by garnering new business from start-up accounts.

8. Gatekeepers are a fact of life and their goal is to keep outsiders out. Make them your best ally. Build a positive relationship with these guardians of the gate.

9. Avoid the fiberglass painted-on-smile and posed, aloof look. Display your "wow" factor by displaying your humanness. Our ability to make ourselves vulnerable is a strong link that binds humanity together.

10. People buy from people they like! Rev up your likeability factor.

"Ignorance is not a virtue."
—Vasillis Katsoulis,
Founder and CEO of Protepo Consulting

CHAPTER SIX
Great Sales Presentations

Presenting your products is more than getting up in front of a potential buyer and reciting a laundry list of features like a robotic talking head. This tinny approach is boring, insulting, and guaranteed to fail. Rather, your task is to create a perceived need for your product within the buyer's mind. Preparation is critical to this process. Enthusiasm, openness, the use of friendly and relaxed presentation techniques, and organization are the keys to a successful outcome. Preparation entails the organization of materials, product knowledge, key benefits and features of your product, along a coherent plan of which features to present first, second, third, and so on.

No one becomes an elite athlete or entertainment star without tremendous practice and preparation. The same is true of a world class salesperson. We are going to assume that you have completed your planning phase for your territory and have gained all the product knowledge you need to proceed. In the event that you haven't completed this preliminary work, your chances for success are slim.

The first phase of planning begins with determining who the prospective client currently uses and why the current vendor is the provider of choice. Then plan your strategic presentation, highlighting the reasons that your product is the better choice. Be cautious and never slam the competition. Save yourself untold heartache in the future by not being antagonistic toward other vendors. You have no way of knowing what relationships exist among your audience with current or potential vendors.

Mental organization is key to success in any type of sales endeavor. Just because you can talk does not mean that you communicate effectively. Disjointed sales points, poorly defined targets, sloppy expression of benefit points, and a lack of knowledge about the buyer can interfere with effective sales communication. Don't fall into the trap of confusing motion with progress or a frenzy of activity with clear-cut results. Choose from your tool kit those features and benefits that specifically apply to your intended audience. Sales presentations are a performance! Adjust your communication skills and presentation points according to the audience receiving the message.

I often get resistance on this point. Typical objections are, "a sale call can't be effective if a canned approach is used" or "I want to be honest and credible." No one is suggesting that you become dishonest or insincere. What is being promoted is that you become so comfortable and fluid with your choice of words that you can pay attention to the non-verbal aspects of the sales call. Great preparation will translate into complete confidence because confidence is a by-product of practice. Practice includes conceptualization, rehearsal, role play, and delivery. People who have achieved success in the Olympics, sports, art entertainment, business, teaching, medicine, research in any field, and so on will tell you that their coaching or training regime was what led to that success.

Sales presentations need to flow smoothly and fluidly with each point leading naturally to the next. You need to consider how the sales points are organized, how benefits are stated, and the order of the material. Techniques that can be used to practice your presentation skills include writing out the sales presentation and clarifying its organization, asking family or friends to critique a verbal presentation or recording the presentation into an audio tape recorder and playing it back. Try to find someone who is not familiar with the products or services you are selling. They can quickly tell you if your presentation makes any sense. Revise your presentation until you are familiar and comfortable with it.

You are now at the point of presenting to someone who understands your industry. Role play to develop your sense of timing and style. Evaluate both the visual and verbal feedback used during the presentation. If at all possible, video tape your presentation. During the playback process you can look at your non-verbal performance. Distracting habits are many and varied. Some distractions to look for include excessive blinking, failure to smile, rigid posture, not looking your audience in the eye, twitching, scratching, fiddling of any kind, playing with pens or pencils, swinging your foot, adjusting neck ties repeatedly, excessive clearing of the throat, and a whole host of other annoying personal quirks or tics. Identify them and get rid of them.

Going Live

You are now ready to take your show on the road. This next step has an almost equal distribution between those sales trainers who suggest that you present first to someone you know versus sales trainers who suggest you present to someone you don't know. I recommend that you opt for what would make you feel the most comfortable, relaxed and confident. If you have no strong preference, choose the most friendly. Remember that customers buy from people they like. Your goal is to become the most likable, expert, organized, helpful salesperson the client has ever met. Following each encounter, analyze your sales presentation. Maintain the techniques, stories, jokes, and words that worked well. Cut out the ones that did not. Keep skillfully crafting your sales presentation words and actions to perfection. Do this, and you will be a winner!

Sales Tools

It is truly difficult to tell your product's story, display its benefits and generate excitement without samples of the product to display to the audience. Facts tell and stories sell. A great many creative methods can be used to highlight how the product or service was developed. Everyone relates to this technique because it is interesting, entertaining, and connects on a deeper level of human understanding.

Sales tools make for far more interesting sales presentations. Buyers respond well to bright, fresh, well presented, informative sales tools. A wide range of tools can be used depending on your industry. If small enough, a new product can be brought to the sales call for show and tell. The client can actually touch the product and pass it around. I have even seen larger items transported on a flat-bed truck so that the potential buyer could have a visual display. Colorful, informative brochures with pictures also work well. Small scale models can also effectively be used and often make great give-aways. Showcasing your wares can be creative and fun.

In some settings an electronic slide deck or video presentation are very effective sales tools. Add a little bit of show business to enhance your presentation. Electronic media is effective for person-to-person or large group presentations. Visual and audio presentations provide the buyer with a more comprehensive understanding of the message you want to showcase. For very small audiences a laptop computer screen can work well. For larger groups a projector and screen are needed. It is best to set up a formal presentation well in advance to ensure that all electronic components are compatible and in good working condition.

Make sure an extra projection bulb is available in case it is needed. It always amazes me what can and will go wrong during a presentation. Equipment fails, extension cords are too short to reach the outlet, fire alarms go off during the presentation, double scheduling of conference space, meetings run over, or your meeting gets reassigned to a new space that won't accommodate your electronic equipment, to name a few. Sage advice is to always have a back-up plan and maintain your sense of humor.

Always have sufficient company literature with you and keep it well organized. Plastic sleeves in a notebook binder can be used to separate and store brochures for easy access. Print materials include company and product brochures, professional article reprints, business cards, and a current client list with up-to-date contact information. Your notebook binder becomes your master sales tool. Keep it filled with company and product literature and keep it up to date. Make certain that you are in compliance with prevailing laws of the country where you are conducting business regarding the use of published materials. Throughout my years of training sales staff, I have come to correlate preparation for the sales call with the salesperson's ability to ultimately succeed. A professional skater can't perform without skates, and a professional salesperson can't perform without a sales kit.

There is not one best system for organizing sales materials. All sorts of systems can work well. Some helpful guidelines include keeping like materials separate from each other so that time is not wasted sorting through a stack of unrelated papers or products to find what you are seeking. Keep those items most frequently used the closet and easiest to retrieve in a hurry. Develop a reliable restocking process. Paper is heavy so a rolling case is easier to handle if you are transporting a significant amount of materials (your back will appreciate the investment).

Keep printed materials current with accurate contact names, phone numbers, websites, and email addresses. If you have had a change in your contact information, print the change out on brightly colored paper with the old information and the new corrected information clearly identified. Add some cartoon work. Cartoons will help get the handout noticed. This will clearly identify your correct and current information. If you have a website, update any changes in contact information. Have changes printed in the company newsletter and displayed on the company website.

Fair or not, we are judged by our appearance and so are our printed materials. Avoid the dog-eared, coffee-stained, or rumpled print materials, and never leave them with a client. Shabby chic may appeal to some individuals as a fashion statement, but it doesn't work in sales. If potential clients judge your materials as substandard, they will automatically judge your services or products as substandard.

Who Controls the Flow?

The client/customer always controls the flow of the sales encounter. That is the way any sales call should be. Build the confidence to let the sales call evolve. There are stylistic choices on how you communicate during the sales encounter. Control is also directly related to how you have built your relationship with the client. The better you know a buyer, the more relaxed and informal you can become and still achieve your sales call objectives. Avoid being presumptuous.

Professionalism is the goal you should strive for in all presentations. Critique your performance after the call while it is still fresh in your mind. Be honest with yourself. Determine what you did well and determine if you need to change or modify any of your presentation.

Jot down what steps you need to take while the call remains fresh in your mind.

What is the most important aspect of a sales call? My answer is always the same: a good sense of humor. When you make a mistake, don't take it too seriously. Retain your personal feeling of self-worth. Self-awareness is vital to any success in life, be it personal beliefs or the development of work-related skills. There will be other calls, other customers, and better days ahead.

KEY POINTS FROM CHAPTER SIX

1. Presenting a product is more than getting in front of a potential buyer and reciting a laundry list of features like a robotic talking head. This approach is guaranteed to fail. Rather, your task is about creating a perceived need for your product or service in the buyer's mind.

2. Much like an elite athlete, no one can become a star salesperson without tremendous practice and preparation. Without preparation your chances of success in the sales arena are slim to none.

3. Mental organization is an important key to success in any type of sales endeavor. Disjointed sales points, poorly defined targets, sloppy expression of benefit points, and a lack of knowledge regarding the buyer or products are all issues that interfere with effective sales results and positive outcomes.

4. Sales presentations are a performance! Adjust your communication skills and presentation points according to the audience receiving the message. The end user wants to know about operating efficiency and how his job will be easier, faster, and safer while finance wants to know the financial impact to the bottom line. Both sets of needs must be effectively addressed.

5. Prepare for the sales call. Become so comfortable and fluid with the presentation that you can pay attention to the non-verbal aspects of the call. Sales presentations need to flow smoothly
.

6. Identify and get rid of distracting habits which are many and varied. Some common ones include excessive blinking, failure to smile, rigid posture, failure to look the audience in the eye, fiddling of any kind with any type of object, excessive clearing of the throat, repeatedly adjusting an article of clothing, and many other personal quirks or tics.

7. Facts tell and stories sell. Tools that can be used effectively to showcase and tell your product's story are well designed and brightly appealing printed brochures and materials, sample products that can be shared with the buyer, electronic slide decks, films, computer animation, and a host of ingenious methods that get the message across in an upbeat, positive way. Be creative and have fun so you captivate your audience.

8. Organize your sales tools. A variety of systems of organization work. There is no correct one way, and you should choose the system that works best for you. Paper and give-aways are heavy. Use a rolling bag for heavy materials.

9. Fair or not, we are judged by our appearance, and that includes our printed material. Avoid

the dog-eared, coffee-stained, or rumpled print materials. If the potential buyer judges your materials as substandard, they will automatically judge your services or products as substandard.

10. The client/customer always controls the flow of the sales encounter. This is the way any sales call should be structured. Build your confidence level to the point that you can let the sales call evolve. The better that you come to know the potential buyer, the more give and take that can develop within the process. Always avoid being presumptuous. And what is the most important aspect of sales calls? A good sense of humor

Dr. Donna Lidga

"There is no substitute for victory."
—General Douglas MacArthur

CHAPTER SEVEN
Generating New Business Accounts
Personal Referrals

There are two tried and true ways to generate new accounts in a given territory. The first is to ask your current accounts for recommendations, referrals, and personal introductions. A positive referral is a gift and should be treated as such. Return the favor as quickly as possible to the individual who recommended you. Often these introductions are made at industry meetings, over lunch, or similar social events. Gathering new business contacts is one of the primary goals of these types of events. Remember that this is an introduction and not a sales call. It is appropriate to exchange business cards or telephone numbers. Call to set up an actual appointment. However, if an actual date and time for meeting is offered, don't hesitate to grab it!

One exception to this rule is direct to consumer sales. When selling direct to an end consumer, it is often best to finalize the sale at the point of contact whenever possible. An example of this type of selling is a person who needs very expensive medication and has a choice of vendors. In this world of complex, high cost, rare disease states, it is best to complete the paperwork as quickly as possible. Since one person can generate hundreds of thousands of dollars in drug costs annually, it is imperative to act quickly and decisively.

There are many industries and products that fall into this category, making product knowledge absolutely essential in the sales process.

Networking calls fall into the realm of personal referrals and can be very worthwhile endeavors. A word of caution is merited here: networking is a two-way process, or in other words, a give and take proposition. Too often networking has been a one sided attempt to get hired, which means that is a time waster and used by individuals who are too lazy to do their own legwork. People's time and energy are just too precious to waste on these people and it is not the role of a networking call to get a new job.

What networking is all about is to use personal contacts to expand business opportunities for each party. For example, one type of networking might be for two independent consultants to refer each other for fulfilling contracts. This is common in the computer industry. Another example would be two or more parties making personal introductions into new accounts or lines of business. I've personally participated in a think tank process, the goal of which was to identify new uses for existing products. The possibilities are limitless, but the process should be a win-win for all parties and tightly controlled. This is a quid-pro-quo activity.

Cold Calling

Cold calling on unknown companies or individuals to determine what business opportunities exist can either be viewed as a grand adventure with pots of gold waiting at the end of the rainbow or a train wreck. There is just no easy way to soften the process. Human beings don't like to be rejected and huge doses of rejection come with this territory. One effective method that I have seen is to do away with the somewhat negative label of cold calls and replace this activity with the phraseology of "market research." This paradigm shift can often make the difference between success and failure.

Ultimately, every person in sales has to develop the prerequisite skills needed to handle this unknown portion of their job to be truly successful. There are some techniques that are helpful to use in attempting to penetrate new accounts. The objective for every customer contact is to gather additional information from face-to-face market research. The goal of all these marketing research calls is face-to-face contact with the potential new client. You are building rapport while gathering useful data.

There are different types of initial contacts that can be used to inform the potential referral source to make them aware of who you are, where you came from, who you represent, and what goods or services your company provides. Since your goal is to gather as much market intelligence on the potential new account as possible, several types of visits or contacts will be required to complete your sales profile. These differing types of calls fall into the categories of:

Introduction/Market Research: Obtain as much working knowledge as you can about the potential account using the same existing account tools previously identified. This technique will make you appear knowledgeable about the opportunity even though you have no prior relationship.

Services Presentation: This presentation can be made from a slide show on a laptop computer, via a sales brochure, or through other types of professional materials. Always leave a behind a document with the salient company points and your business contact information.

Follow-up/Servicing Calls: The goal of any contact is to obtain another appointment or contact for follow-up. Follow-up calls are critical to long term successful relationships. One successful method is to listen for the client's needs or ask the potential client what you could provide them that would help move their business along. Once again, you are establishing a helpful relationship, credibility, and displaying your level of consistency at this point of the process.

Education/In-services: In some highly technical sales situations, one technique that can be very effective at getting invited to present in front of the staff is to make a presentation to key members on relevant topics. In many fields annual continuing education credits are required. Have your presentation accredited by the appropriate agency that grants continuing education units for your industry so that attendees can meet continuing education credits requirements for the year. Use the question and answer period to weave in facts about your company and its goods and services. It is often this type of soft selling venue that will get you an appointment with the purchasing agent.

Not all opportunities are created equal. Once you have completed your due diligence on a potential new account, you are ready to determine its efficacy in the marketplace. After determining the quantification and qualification of each new account, the last step is to determine if the account is worth pursuing, and if it is, how much of your time you should devote to the account. The pitfall at this stage of the sales process is to spend too much time and too many resources on low yield opportunities and too little time on accounts with high yield potential. Being subject to human emotions, we often base time allocation decisions on who we like to be around. Time is money. Spend it wisely on referral sources with large potential results.

A Season for Everything

Either a need exists for your services or it doesn't. Because a need doesn't exist today doesn't mean that it will never exist. There are several steps to take that will keep your company and your name in front of this group. Put them on your email list for company press releases and other company sanctioned emails. Add them to the company newsletter list. Call and check-in every three months. Visit and refresh company literature once every six months. Briefly inform potential clients of any new or expanded services. Ask if there is anything you can provide them and make certain you follow-up. When a need does arise, you will not be a stranger to them as you have already established that you are a reliable and, valid resource for their business needs.

If you are trying hard to obtain the account because of its potential added volume of business in your territory, then you can up the ante. If you send flowers for the office, send them not at holidays where they tend to get lost with everyone else's, but during an off-time when they will stand out. This same process works for most all office-type gifts. If you are wooing a particular person, find out what that person would really appreciate, such as hard-to-get sports or event tickets. Send at least two tickets with a note that you were thinking of them and hope they enjoy the event. The point is to keep the gift reasonable and gear it towards what the potential client likes. Strike a balance by not going overboard and not coming across as cheap. A word of caution: some industries have stringent guidelines regarding gift giving. Know the rules of your particular business setting, country, and industry. Fines and penalties can be stiff for violators.

KEY POINTS FROM CHAPTER SEVEN

1. There are several tried and true ways to generate new business sales accounts in a given territory. The first is to ask current account managers who already do business with you for a personal introduction to potential new customers. These introductions often take place at social events, community service club meetings, or industry-sponsored shows.

2. Networking calls also fall into the category of personal referrals and can be very effective. Networking is a give and take process. Networking is not intended solely to further your career, nor is networking one-sided. Both parties give to get. Many business consortiums are formed around networks to everyone's benefit and profit.

3. Direct to consumer sales is, in many ways, an exception to the process of working a potential account. Often the consumer is actually the decision maker based on very high dollar volumes and rarity of their medical condition associated with their care and treatment. Competition is brutal, so process the sale as quickly as possible.

4. Cold calls can either be viewed as a grand adventure with pots of gold at the end of the rainbow or a train wreck. No one enjoys the sting of being rejected. It is a helpful technique

to re-label cold calling as "market research." This paradigm shift allows you to build rapport while gathering useful data. This technique allows you to build a relationship before you attempt the sales process and it is always easier to sell to who you know. Get to know prospective customers.

5. Several different types of initial contacts are used to make the potential client aware of who you are, where you came from, who you represent, and what goods and services your company provides. Initial contacts fall into the categories of introduction/market research; introduction of company services, follow-up calls, and education/in-services.

6. There is a season for everything. Either a need exists for your services or it doesn't. Because a need doesn't exist today does not mean that it will never exist. Keep working the account.

7. Establish yourself as a valid resource that can be counted on to be reliable in meeting future business needs.

8. Gift giving is a standard practice in sales. The gift should be reasonable and geared towards the particular client's preferences. Strike a balance between cheapness and going overboard. Research and know your industry's, and your country's rules and regulations, regarding gift giving to avoid inadvertently

violating laws. Penalties are often very expensive.

9. Electronic media is increasing our global contacts, opening new opportunities, and enhancing our sales numbers. Learn how to tap into this valuable new marketing tool.

10. Network as often as possible in as many networking forums that are available to you in your assigned territory. Personal contact remains one of the "gold standards" of sales.

Dr. Donna Lidga

"Success isn't a result of spontaneous combustion. You must set yourself on fire."
—Arnald H. Glasgow

CHAPTER EIGHT
Value-added Selling

A successful sale is about telling the customer what they want to hear. Your task is to present information in your own unique form and style that best suits your personality, while at the same time meeting the needs of the customer. Your goal is to establish a need in the mind of the buyer.

Value added selling is governed by several marketplace conditions. It is particularly needed in the following scenarios:

When the marketplace is saturated with products and prices that are highly competitive: Competition surrounding similar products in the marketplace will force constant downward pressure on prices and drive innovation through the need for constant creative product development.

When there is a diminished need for effective sales skills: When customers have a large number of companies to choose from which all offer the same products and services, the need for effective sales skills is diluted. This is particularly true when price, product, and services are similar. If all you give to potential customers is "buzz" words, you will sound just like everyone else. When you become part of the background noise, it will be easy to tune you out.

If your sales presentation states the obvious and does not define the unique value you offer, then the obvious becomes meaningless to the potential buyer.

Adding Value

The premise of value-added selling is to establish a perceived need in the mind of the buyer. In order to create the perceived value, you must first realistically define what value means to the buyer. The activity of studying people and their quirks is one of the more fun aspects of selling. It is all about understanding what motivates people to do what they do. Perceived value is unique to different buyers and can vary wildly within a given company. This means that a salesperson must always know who the target audience is and who the final decision maker is. The Chief Operating Officer has a different agenda than the department head, whose job differs still from the purchasing agent, who deviates from the end user. Even within family structures one partner is usually the dominant decision maker. The level of dominance can shift depending on the purchase being considered.

Value is married to worth. Wed your products or services to the worth that your potential customer seeks. Keep in mind that each customer can seek a different aspect of worth. The concept of value added is perceptual. In reality many companies provide the same or similar products. What makes an end user buy one product over another? It is because the purchaser perceives more value from one vendor over the other.

Value can be real or perceived. Some common buying themes emerge to provide a guidepost for the salesperson along the way (these are not listed in any particular order of importance):

Comfort provided to the purchaser: The phrase "no worries buying" applies here. The buyer does not have to worry whether or not a good job is being done. This can take a huge burden off the plate of many stressed-out buyers. You are making the customer's life easier and you will get a lot of repeat business as a result.

Product technology: Zero in on how your product can perform in the marketplace. Any aspect can be touted here from size, weight, durability, visual appeal, ease of use, new avenues of usage, color, broader base of appeal, and so forth. What you are providing in reality are the keys to successfully marketing the product and increasing sales.

Profit: Cost is a fairly straight forward issue. When the products you are selling fall into the same range as the competition, look for the value added metrics, either real or perceived. These can be product technology, scope of services, education, or licensing parameters, to name a few.

Response time and other services: Time is money. If you can deliver your products faster and cheaper, you'll have a leg up on the competition. Reliability is one of those non-negotiable traits and can often separate the sheep from the goats. Strive in every way possible to be reliable. Return phone calls, answer emails, and keep appointments.

Fear: Fear is a definite factor in buying decisions. Fear is often subliminal and extremely powerful as a motivator. The fear factor may be hidden and sneaks in as a "what if." TV ads make good use of this psychological hook as evidenced by certain ads. Picture the commercial featuring tires that perform well in rainy driving conditions when a mother drives with young children on board. Or the insurance commercial touting offers of protection for sudden accidents or even death benefits for survivors. You will notice the heavy use of phrases like "offers protection" and "keep your loved ones safe." There are numerous examples to choose from that use this technique.

Trust: It is hard to build and easy to lose. Stay focused on your client's needs and your client's profit margins. Be prepared to discuss cost factors in realistic terms. Value-added selling goes hand in glove with the service component of selling. Business building requires that you face honestly what is the most appropriate action and take that action. Short cuts often lead to dishonesty, inappropriate business practices, dismissal from the company, or even jail time.

Organizing Your Sales Presentation

Organize your sales presentation around the value topics that your potential buyer needs to hear. Most often your audience will be looking toward their own personal convenience in handling your products, cost comparisons, elimination of fear factors (either real or contrived), and meeting any regulatory requirements. To be effective in meeting these value needs you must do the following:

- Establish value in the buyer's mind. Never assume that the buyer knows the value of your products.

- Define your commodity through the product's quality.

- Be prepared to proactively discuss the cost of your products.

- Make certain that perception and reality are the same.

Be prepared to rationally and calmly explain how you and your company are better prepared to provide these services than anyone else. Stress the value that you bring to the sales process. You will always want to stress the benefits that you offer and remember that perceived benefits can vary widely. Know who your audience is and meet your target audience's needs. The success of a given sales call is to address the features and benefits to this specific buyer. Many novice sales personnel get his or her personal needs all mixed up with the client's desires. Your goal is to meet your potential clients needs not stroke your own ego. This issue can be a very real stumbling block if the salesperson had any role in product development. Check your ego at the door.

Due to the limited amount of time allotted to sales calls, it is a helpful technique to present your top three selling points at the beginning of your presentation. This will ensure that you stress your strongest selling points first. However, always come prepared to address all your selling points, because sometimes the persuading benefit for the purchaser may not reside in your top benefits. Something lower down the list might solve a very real business problem that the potential client is experiencing. These problems could include packaging, delivery times, consistent product availability, weight that lowers shipping and handling costs, bold new design, fresh appealing colors, improved efficiency or effectiveness, etc.

Success in benefit selling is linked to your ability to prioritize features and benefits to each specific buying source. Your goal is to convince the buyer that you and your company offer value at a competitive price. Value, price, and innovation are a winning combo every time.

KEY POINTS FROM CHAPTER EIGHT

1. The goal of benefit selling is to establish a need in the mind of the buyer for your product or service.

2. Value-added selling is governed by market conditions wherein the marketplace is saturated with similar products: as a result, price levels are highly competitive.

3. Competition surroundings similar products in the marketplace will force constant downward pressure on prices and drive innovation through the need to continually seek the creative edge.

4. If all you have to offer a potential customer is "buzz" words, you will sound just like everyone else. When you become part of the background noise, it will be easy to tune you out.

5. Your goal is to establish value-added presentations and selling tools. The premise of value-added selling is to establish a perceived need in the mind of the buyer. Perceived value is unique to different buyers and can vary wildly within a given company. You must always know your target audience.

6. Value is married to worth. Wed your products or services to the perception of what your client seeks. The concept of value is perceptual.

7. Comfort with "no worries buying," product technology, profit margins, response times, lessening fear factors, and building trust are all value-added selling concepts. Each has many components to explore in making your sales presentations.

8. Establish value in the buyer's mind. Never assume that a buyer knows the value of your products.

9. The goal of a given sales call is to address the features and benefits to this specific buyer. Not everyone in the organization is seeking the same features and outcomes. Become astute at identifying who has purchasing authority.

10. Success in benefit selling is linked to your ability to prioritize features and benefits. Your goal is to convince the buyer that you and your company offer value at a competitive price. Value and price win every time.

"No rules for success will work if you don't."
—Universal Wisdom

CHAPTER NINE
Pulling It Together: Dynamic Openings, Managing Objections, and Great Closings

Congratulations you have arrived at the moment of truth. It is time for action. For the sake of clarity and ease of discussion, I have broken the sales process into four sequential components:

- Opening
- Discussion
- Managing Objections
- Closing/Follow-up

In the real world, objections are often voiced early in the discussion. The inability to successfully handle objections in a positive way often determines the ultimate success or failure of the sales call. Being able to respond positively to objections is one of the barriers that your hours of rehearsal and preparation will have prepared you to effectively handle in a positive manner.

Objectives of a Sales Call

Each sales call has objectives to fulfill. There are three common objectives for working a new account:

Discuss your service or products so that there is an identifiable outcome. This step is meant to create interest in your product or services and get invited back to make a formal presentation. Have follow-up topics to discuss in the event the referral source doesn't have an interest in your preliminary subject.

Gather additional information about the customer and the business. Seek information germane to your ultimate goal. Collect company literature, talk to the support staff, ask questions, and show your genuine interest.

Arrange an appointment for your next visit. Create reasons to continue the discussion. Offer to provide additional material or research an identified problem. Always end with a statement like: "When would be a good time for me to make a follow up appointment?" Don't leave the premises without that next appointment in your calendar!

Effective Openings

This step sets the stage for the entire sales call. Paramount to this approach is establishing good rapport with your customer and setting the stage. This allows you to be yourself so that you come across as relaxed, engaging, and friendly. Appropriate topics include sports, weather, current events, common friends, etc. Always talk about what the customer wants to talk about. While this type of chatter is important, be cautious that it doesn't dominate your entire allotted time slot. At times these social topics can be tricky. For example, if you are not a huge sports fan it is best to disarm any tension around this topic early on. One smooth method is to have a couple of well rehearsed lines that disarms the situation by poking fun at yourself. Another technique that I have seen used with great success by men is claiming they are color blind when it comes to shopping of any kind. Almost everyone can relate to this comment with a smile. Sometimes it is even true!

Stay in Control, and Set the Direction

Use these two verbal techniques to effectively set the stage to take the sales call in the right direction:

Start your discussion with a general benefit statement about your service or product that garners the customer's attention. One helpful technique so that you don't leave anything of importance out of your presentation is to jot down the key benefits in outline form on a cheat sheet that only you see. This will keep your presentation focused and on track.

Ask the customer what his greatest need is in relationship to your service or product. This technique is a little harder to control and master, but it is powerful in that it engages the customer in the sales process from the very opening statement. It is important to use an open-ended question that requires the potential customer to respond in statement format as opposed to using a yes or no answer that allows the conversation to die out.

By prompting dialogue you can gain valuable information in two ways. First, you are establishing rapport with the customer. Second, you are learning how your potential customer makes decisions.

Everyone has opinions. Your goal is to get your potential buyer to share his or her opinion with you.

Sales discussions are, in fact, sales interviews. The listen/talk ratio of a good sales call is one wherein the customer does 60% or more of the talking.

A valid question is which opening technique works best under what type of circumstances. The rule of thumb used to address this dilemma is as follows:

- With commodity products that are well known, use general benefits as your selling approach.

- With conceptualization products/services, the use of open-ended benefits works well.

- With both techniques it is extremely important not to come across as contrived or patronizing, either of which is a kiss of death.

Managing Objections

In all my years of managing people across a wide spectrum of industries, I've yet to meet anyone who enjoys rejection or hasn't experienced issues in effectively learning to deal with this stinging nettle. The black shroud of handling rejection has fallen upon all of us at one time or another. The only way to effectively handle this thorny issue is to separate the personal self from the sales process. The customer is not rejecting you personally. Customers disagree with what you are saying for three primary reasons:

- A lack of information or a misunderstanding of your product

- Resistance to change
- Disbelief in your company

In sales, you will encounter all of these types of rejection at one time or another in your career. It is the nature of business and it is not personal. On the other hand, personal rejections do occur. No one likes everyone they meet. A personal rejection will be quite apparent to you. One of two things will occur. Either the client will tell you what he doesn't like about you, or, he will refuse to see you again. Either way, the message is crystal clear.

Two courses of action are usually open to you at this stage. One is to salvage the account if at all possible and the second is to turn the account over to someone else to manage if you can't salvage the account through damage control. Learn from the situation and move on. It happens to all of us in some form throughout our lives, ergo, it happens to all of us who sell. Life is too short to dwell on the negative. Choose the positive path and move on. It is guaranteed that new opportunities will present themselves along the way. Learn from the situation, be prepared, and be ready for the next opportunity. If you stay stuck in the past, you'll never be ready for the future.

What Is the Process for Managing Objections?

All humans have perspectives that are just plain lacking in logic. You and I are not exceptions to this rule. It helps to frame a "crazy," non-factual opinion by remembering that all of us fall into this trap to a greater or lesser depth at one time or another. The temptation is always to get defensive and defend your position. Resist the temptation and don't lash out because this approach is guaranteed to lead to disaster every time. Here are some steps to assist you in handling this type of situation:

Relax: Take a deep breath and avoid striking back.

Clarify the objection: Most of the time, the client will start with a broad, open-ended statement that truly doesn't address the under lying complaint. A common example is, "I've always had problems with your company." Your next step is to dig deeper to uncover the true objection. Once you know what the true issue or problem is you can begin to resolve it.

Answer the objection: If you know the answer to the problem being identified, let the client know the answer and make certain that the customer is satisfied with the explanation. If you are unfamiliar with the issue that the customer raises, inform the customer that you will investigate the issue and return with an answer in a reasonable timeframe. It is absolutely imperative to stay on schedule and communicate with the customer even if it is to provide a status report update and to set a new date for final resolution. Customers aren't unreasonable about timeframes, but no one appreciates hanging out in the wind not knowing what is happening. Keep the information flowing!

Continue your presentation: Once you have established a plan of action then continue with your sales presentation.

All sorts of issues can muddy the mix when dealing with objections. Common themes that result in confusion include past versus future events and placing blame versus accepting responsibility. You are not required to accept blame for events that happened in the past if you were not directly involved. It is, however, your role to accept responsibility in resolving the problems now and in the future. Keeping these concepts straight in your mind can save you much grief and many sleepless nights. As a rule of thumb, if your client offers you an opportunity to prove him wrong, then his objections are opportunities in disguise.

Strong Closings

Believe it or not, the timing and nuisances around effective techniques of closing a sales call can be among the most difficult to learn and to execute smoothly. All sorts of human behavior can come into play surroundings the closing process, some funny and many painful. Through the years I have had new employees exhibit a wide gamut of behavior. One person just abruptly stated that he had nothing more to say and sat down with every eye in the meeting staring at him. At the other end of the spectrum, one young lady just couldn't stop talking even when she clearly was beginning to deviate from the sales process into revealing personal information. Both events required rescue.

Fear is often the barrier that prevents people from being effective closers. Fear is based on perceptions, and if the perception is incorrect, a positive outcome is at risk. Common inappropriate perceptions are:

Fear of not being accepted by the customer: Rejection is a strong and powerful fear for human beings. To counter this fundamental fear effectively, you must understand and grasp that the role of a salesperson is not to win a popularity contest. Everyone desires to be liked but you are striving for respect in your role of sales. You gain and retain respect by telling the truth. Humans simply do not like change. Research has shown that nine out of ten people will not change even if they are provided with the facts, experience fear, or are subjected to force. This fact is the most compelling argument to developing a sound sales plan. Otherwise you are playing the game of "wing-it."

Fear of a knowledge deficit: It is true that product knowledge is the key to sales success. However, it is nearly impossible for any of us to have complete and total knowledge about every subject. We live in a world of instant communication wherein new knowledge is being added every second. The most effective way to deal with this is to understand that all of us are in the same jet being propelled forward at rocket speeds. Learn to say, "I don't know the answer to that question, but I'll find out and get back to you." I've used this approach many times and it is almost always effective. I've even had customers smile and tell me that the issue wasn't "real" and that they just wanted to determine how honest I was. In this case, it's okay to mentally think "jerk" smile, and move on!

Lack of preparation: This one is simple. If you do not believe in or understand your product or service then you cannot defend it. If this is caused by a training deficit you can take corrective action and expand your knowledge base. If you truly don't believe in the products or services you are selling, it is time to look for another job. Staying under these circumstances does no one any positive good, not you, and not the company who employs you.

❖ When to close is always situational. Look for both non-verbal and verbal buying signals.

❖ Non-verbal buying signals from the potential buyer include:

- Smiling
- Nodding
- Leaning forward towards you

Verbal buying signals include when the customer:

- States a specific use for your product within the organization
- Asks how quickly something can be done or delivered
- Calls in a colleague to hear about the product or pricing
- Asks about your buying service requirements
- Makes a positive statement
- Asks about the track record of similar customers

Pay close attention for these clues. Don't be a non-observant salesperson that snatches defeat from the jaws of victory! Closing is a request for action. It's your job to take that action.

KEY POINTS FROM CHAPTER NINE

1. Each sales call has an objective to fulfill. Three common objectives are to discuss your products or services with an identifiable outcome, to gather additional information about the customer's business, and to arrange for the next visit.

2. Effective openings set the stage for the entire sales call. Paramount to this approach is to establish good rapport with the customer. Setting the stage allows you to be yourself so that you can come across as relaxed, engaging, and friendly.

3. Always, talk about what the customer wants to talk about. Social chatter is extremely important to setting the stage, but beware of this process taking over the sales process. Be prepared with a couple of smooth lead-ins to the actual sales presentation.

4. Two verbal techniques that are effective in leading into the sales discussion are to pose a general benefit statement or ask the customer to identify his greatest need in relation to your services or products. Learn when it is most appropriate to use these techniques.

5. Sales discussions are, in fact, sales interviews. The client should do 60% of the talking. You gain valuable information from this process.

6. Managing objections is an art form. No one enjoys rejection. Rejection can be quite painful and it is difficult not to personalize the process. Customers disagree with what you are saying for three primary reasons: a lack of information or a misunderstanding of your product, resistance to change, and disbelief in your company.

7. There is a process for managing objections. Relax and avoid striking back, clarify the objection, answer the objection if you can, promise to research the answer if you don't know, and continue with your presentation. It is vital that you maintain control of the sales process and learn how to effectively handle these disruptions without being side-tracked.

8. Strong closings require skills that must be honed in order to execute smoothly. All sorts of human behavior can come into play surrounding the closing process, some funny and some painful. Fear is usually the barrier that prevents people from being effective closers.

9. Fear is based on perceptions. Common inappropriate perceptions include a fear of not being accepted, a fear of knowledge deficits and a fear of inadequate preparation.

10. When closing your presentation, you should look for both verbal and non-verbal buying clues. Non-verbal clues include smiling,

nodding, and leaning forward. Verbal buying clues include requests for specific outcomes by the potential buyer such as how to place orders, delivery times, billing and payment terms, etc. Closing is a request for action. Seize the victory!!

"Where you start is not as important as where you finish."

—Zig Ziglar

CHAPTER TEN
International Sales

Of all the paradigm shifts of the past twenty plus years, none have been as dramatic as the shift from a national to a global economy. Vast new world markets for goods and services have opened up. Several factors have fueled this growth, the most notable being instant communication via the internet. The internet is fast, cheap, and easy to use. The convergence of these three attributes has touched all aspects of our lives. It has also forced commerce, business, and the provision of services in totally new directions, and has placed new and often unfamiliar demands on companies and their employees.

What is extremely interesting is that the challenges to navigate successfully in these new waters are not limited to the buyers, sellers, or consumers. A paradigm shift of this magnitude has many subsets associated with it and impacts the very fabric of a culture. Underpinning these paradigm shifts is an incredibility enhanced timeline for change. Changes that in the past took decades to impact the business model can now occur in only a very few short weeks or months. Small family-owned and managed businesses find it harder and harder to survive and compete due to the globalization of business. On the flip side of this paradigm shift is the creation of new avenues to market all sorts of new durable goods and services to an ever increasing and hungry global marketplace. Beware that rapid growth can place additional strain on any type of business, service, or market.

Many countries do not have well trained, professional managers who can be counted on to successfully lead the new and more complex business model. In more industrialized countries the training of new managers follows a logical sequence of steps geared to provide experience in increasingly complex positions of authority. The growth curves of emerging countries and economies often outstrip the ability to train and the amount of time required to stabilize the need for managers and leaders.

This factor can often be an area of entry into the new market. A savvy company can use its own expertise as the entry point by providing managerial support to assist in the purchase and distribution of goods in a constructive and supportive manner. Sales personnel often fill in the gap of missing skills. Today's modern world is both helpful and potentially harmful. Toxic political structures that lead to corruption and the widespread practice of graft also have a deleterious effect on new business opportunities.

So how does all of this impact sales? For a company to be successful in sales, the company has to be prepared to compete more, not less, in the emerging global economy. As a consequence, many salespeople will have to be equally prepared to sell globally. Many types of sales can be handled exclusively via internet using international shipping and revenue collection services. Other types of sales will require person-to-person contact. Person-to-person contact requires a whole new set of social skills, etiquette, overcoming language barriers, time zones, jet lag, dress codes, gift giving, conversation dos and don'ts, etc.

Fortunately, many guides exist to aid a salesperson venturing into an uncharted territory. The evaluation and preparation related to working new accounts in other countries are essentially the same as the process used in one's home territory, although additional research will be required in the area of cultural attributes. There are some excellent resources available for researching various areas of the globe. Listed below are just some of the good sources of information about world customs available to you. This is by no means an exhaustive list, but is meant to be a tasty tidbit of all the information that is available to you with a little research.

Conde Nast Traveler

The internet
"Business Travel Etiquette" by Arizona State University in Tempe, Arizona.
Available at: <Libguides.asu.edu/intletiq>.

"Business Travel Etiquette" available at:
<buzzle.com>.

"The Knowledge Creating Company" by Britt Institute.
Available at: <www.pegasusconsultants.com>.

"Teaching Professionals to Outclass Their Competition" by the Lett Group. Available at:
<info@lettgroup.com>.

Protocol Teasers

Each region of the world has uniqueness to offer. It is what makes travel so very compelling and interesting. Travel also rounds us out as human beings, exposes us to new methods of doing routine tasks like eating and dressing, and shows us that many varying approaches can be successfully used to accomplish the same tasks. One of my most engaging and interesting friends has traveled to all seven continents. She is a wealth of stories and anecdotes, some funny, others inspiring, and all informative.

Travel Tidbits and Teasers

Color: Something as simple as color can be significant. For instance, in China the color red is considered a lucky color. Red was worn by Chinese athletes in the Olympics and the Chinese wear red wedding dresses. Tiger Woods wears red on the last day of a golf tournament for luck. Psychologists have demonstrated that teams that wear red uniforms score an average of 13% more points than teams who wear blue uniforms.

On the flip side, at her husband's victory rally, Michelle Obama and her two daughters were criticized by the American press for wearing dresses that were black and red in color. As it turns out, black and red are mourning colors in Africa and the Obama family was paying respect for President Obama's recently deceased grandmother. On the other hand, red is considered a powerful color in the United States and Michelle

Obama wears red quite often. Sometimes customs don't follow logic.

Food

Food is universal. Everyone has to eat in order to survive. However, the way we eat and what we eat varies considerably. The act of sharing a meal is steeped in cultural norms and customs. Religious beliefs influence our preparation and consumption of food. Among my friends, co-workers, and acquaintances, I can always tell how much someone enjoyed a new type of cuisine by their weight gain or loss following a long trip! The type of food, its preparation, and sharing mealtime customs should be researched thoroughly before taking a trip to a new country.

In some countries food is ordered communally and shared, but even within this custom the presentation of food can vary significantly. In China food if often ordered in advance of a business meeting, while some African countries use large platters laden with several varying types of food to serve everyone seated at the table. Sanitation in some countries is more lax than others, which includes the handling and storage of food. Research food handling standards completely and follow strict health guidelines. Bottled water has definitely made safe drinking water easier to obtain. Pageantry often surrounds business deals, so familiarize yourself with the process in advance. Through common sense and by following a few basic hygiene rules, international travel becomes fascinating, mind expanding, and enjoyable.

Tipping

Tipping etiquette also varies significantly around the globe. The best approach is to buy a tipping guide and study it in advance of your trip. One of the strangest customs that I encountered in my travels had to do with having to pay for toilet paper before using the toilets. In countries that don't have many indigenous trees, the cost of toilet paper is very high, therefore its use is tightly controlled. I learned quickly to bring flat rolls of toilet paper, hand wipes, and a backpack for carrying all my supplies with me. Even the design of toilets can be a challenge for the unsuspecting!

Hand Gestures

Hand gestures are a large part of how any culture communicates. Hand gestures are so commonplace that it is easy to forget their significance until you get that "glazed over" look when someone gives you a gesture that you don't know how to interpret, or don't know whether a response is expected. If you're not prepared, you won't know what is expected of you. Hand gestures are all about personal space and saving face. If all else fails, just laugh at yourself and admit that you don't understand what to do. Some kind soul is bound to come to your rescue to help diffuse the situation.

Final Tips

Finding your place in the world is important. Too many people in our incredibly fast-paced, modern world are adrift with no sense of purpose. Anger, frustration, and confusion abound. People feel betrayed by governments, businesses, and institutions of all types. The future seems unknown and unknowable. At this stage of the shifting paradigm, there exist more questions than answers. Now is the time to bond to your higher purpose, your family, your friends, and your life's work. Invent your own future. Remember your time is your dime. Use your time wisely.

Grand Finale

Included is a worksheet that you can use as a guide in your research of any global location. I would encourage you to use the guide and do your due diligence before you accept an assignment in any unfamiliar part of the globe. The blocking and tackling of travel can present a myriad of challenges. Preparation will prevent you from unraveling and spinning out of control.

Happy selling!

SAMPLE WORKSHEET FOR A NEW MARKET

Name:
Address:

Contact Information:
Phone:
Cell Phone:

Country Being Profiled:

PLEASE PROVIDE AS MUCH DETAIL AS POSSIBLE.

This questionnaire is intended as a guide only. Please feel free to add valuable insights and information for anyone wanting to do business in a new market. Each cell will expand to accommodate the length of each response.

Traditions

Question: What traditions of the country should a visitor observe?
Response:

Question: What is the proper way to greet the following people?

Dignitaries:
Superiors:
Peers:

Working class:
Field Specialists:
Opposite Sex:
Children:
Elderly:

Question: What is proper professional etiquette?
Response:

Question: What is proper social etiquette?
Response:

Question: What is the proper way to address the following people?

Dignitaries:
Superiors:
Peers:
Field Specialists:
Working class:
Opposite Sex:
Children:
Elderly:

Question: Which American traditions are or would be viewed negatively?
Response:

Question: Which American behaviors are or would be viewed negatively?
Response:

Question: What are acceptable business gifts? Food, flowers, candy, booze, books? Identify any additional appropriate items.
Response:

Question: What holidays (religious and national) are observed? How is business/sales viewed during these holidays?

Response:

Religion

Question: What is the dominate religion of the country?
Response:

Question: What other faiths are prominent in the country?
Response:

Question: Are there any religious observations that one should be aware of?
Response:

Question: Does Religion have a place in business transactions?
Response:

Question: Are there religious practices that are honored at the workplace?
Response:

Question: What impact do religious observations have at the workplace?
Response:

Language

Question: What English words should be avoided that would resemble a word in the native language that would be vulgar or offensive?
Response:

Question: Who can act as an interpreter?
Response:

Legal

Question: What are the entry requirements in the country? Visa? Passport?
Response:

Question: Are special clearances required to enter different parts of the country?
Response:

Question: What currencies are accepted?
Response:

Question: Are there restricted areas of the country?
Response:

Question: Are passports surrendered at hotels?
Response:

Culture

Question: What language (s) is spoken?
Response:

Question: What does a visitor need to know about human contact between members of the same sex? The opposite sex?
Response:

Question: What foods are considered taboo or unacceptable to eat?
Response:

Agriculture/Industry

Question: What is the primary industry?
Response:

Question: What are the leading agricultural products?
Response:

Question: What are the leading industrial products?
Response:

Question: What are the leading reasons for tourism?
Sightseeing:
Art:
Architecture:
History:
Recreational Activities:
Night Life:
Other:

Etiquette

Question: What verbal greeting is appropriate when first meeting your customer, client, or vendor?
Response:

Question: What physical greeting is appropriate for each? Hand shake, hug, bow, etc?
Response:

Question: What are the traditional/religious guidelines for physical contact?
Response:

Question: Is hand-to-hand contact forbidden?
Response:

Question: Is hand-to-hand contact with a certain hand forbidden?
Response:

Question: What is the appropriate demeanor when meeting the following people?
A Receptionist:
A Guide:
A Counterpart:
A Field Specialist:
A Departmental Executive:
A Board Member:
A Top Level Executive:

Question: Is it appropriate to give a gift?
Response:

Question: To whom is it appropriate to give a gift?
Response:

Question: What type of gift is appropriate to give?
Response:

Question: What type of gift is not appropriate to give?
Response:

Question: Are certain types of gifts taboo? Like alcohol?
Response:

Question: Is there symbolism for certain kinds of gifts?
Response:

Question: Is giving flowers appropriate?
Response:

Question: In a business setting, to whom is it appropriate to present flowers?
Response:

Question: In a business setting, what types of flowers are appropriate?
Response:

Question: Is there symbolism for certain types of flowers?
Response:

Question: Are certain flower types to be avoided because of a traditional meaning? Is there a flower that symbolizes mourning/death? Or romance?
Response:

Question: Is direct eye contact appropriate?
Response:

Business & Social Follow-up: Lunch

Question: What are the rules of lunch dining etiquette?
Response:

Question: Are certain foods considered finger-food?
Response:

Question: If alcoholic beverages are offered, what are the traditional rules governing acceptance or non-acceptance?
Response:

Question: If a choice of a seat is your decision, where should you seat yourself in relation to your guide, counterpart, president, departmental executive?
Response:

Question: Are there any negative superstitions to avoid which may have an impact on your image/relationship or which may be a sign of bad luck?
Response:

Question: Are there customs to observe when entering an eating establishment? Like removing your shoes?
Response:

Question: What foods and beverages should you expect to be offered?
Response:

Question: What foods and beverages should you avoid?
Response:

Question: Is there conversation during the meal?
Response:

Question: Will business be discussed during the meal?
Response:

Question: Is there a time before, during or after the meal when business would be discussed?
Response:

Question: What type of conversation should you be prepared for during the meal?
Response:

Question: What topics should be avoided during the meal?
Response:

Question: When is it considered appropriate to accept a meal or to pay for a meal?
Response:

Question: With whom should you expect to dine?
Response:

Question: If your meal is "serve yourself" from a selection of items, what quantity is considered appropriate?
Response:
Business & Social Follow-up: Dinner

Question: What are the rules of dinner dining etiquette?
Response:

Question: Is there appropriate attire for dinner?
Response:

Question: Are certain foods considered finger-food?
Response:

Question: If alcoholic beverages are offered, what are the traditional rules governing acceptance or non-acceptance?
Response:

Question: If a choice of a seat is your decision, where should you seat yourself in relation to your guide, counterpart, president, departmental executive?
Response:

Question: Are there any negative superstitions to avoid which may have an impact on your image/relationship, be a sign of bad luck, etc.?
Image:
Relationship:
Be a sign of bad luck:
Other:

Question: Are there customs to observe when entering an eating establishment? Like removing one's shoes?
Response:

Question: What foods and beverages should you expect to be offered?
Response:

Question: What foods and beverages should you avoid?
Response:

Question: Is there conversation during the meal?
Response:

Question: Will business be discussed during the meal?
Response:

Question: Is there a time when business would be discussed?
Response:

Question: What type of conversation should you be prepared for during the meal?
Response:

Question: What topics should be avoided during the meal?
Response:

Question: When is it considered appropriate to accept a meal or to pay for the meal?
Response:

Question: With whom would you expect to dine?
Response:

Question: From whom do you take your lead to begin eating?
Response:

Question: If your meal is "serve yourself" from a selection of items, what quantity is considered appropriate?
Response:

Question: Is there any action during the meal that might be considered insulting to your dinner partners?
Response:

Receptions

Question: What is the appropriate attire for a reception?
Response:

Question: Can you expect a receiving line?
Response:

Question: How should you pay your respects to your host at the reception?
Response:

Question: What would be your demeanor toward a spouse?
Response:

Question: Where would you expect a reception to take place?
Response:

Question: Is a gift appropriate for the host?
Response:

Question: Is a gift appropriate for the hostess?
Response:

Question: Is a gift appropriate for both?
Response:

Question: What type of gift would be appropriate for a host?
Response:

Question: What type of gift would be appropriate for a hostess?
Response:

Question: What type of gift would be appropriate for both?
Response:

Question: What type of gift should be avoided?
Response:

Question: Are flowers appropriate?
Response:

Question: Do types of flowers carry a special meaning that should be considered?
Response:

Question: Is it expected to discuss business at a reception?
Response:

Question: Are there topics of conversation to be avoided?
Response:

The Next Day

Question: How does the next day start?
Response:
Question: Will you dine before meeting?
Response:
Question: Will they normally pick you up?
Response:

Question: If you dine together, should you offer to pay?
Response:

Question: If you are offered something that you feel would be an imposition, should you accept or decline?
Response:

Question: Are there certain customs that would guide the decision to accept or decline?
Response:

Question: How personal/familiar should a relationship become?
Response:

Question: Would behaviors be different if you are a top executive?
Response:

Question: Would behaviors be different if you are a
middle level executive?
Response:

Question: Would behaviors be different if you are a
field specialist?
Response:

Please list any further questions or information that you
feel would be helpful to a person or company doing
business in the country:

Question:
Response:

Question:
Response:

Question:
Response:

Question:
Response:

Question:
Response:

Question:
Response:

Question:
Response:

Additional Comments:

_____
_____
_____
_____
_____
_____
_____
_____
_____
_____
_____
_____
_____
_____
_____
_____
_____
_____
_____
_____
_____
_____
_____
_____
_____
_____
_____
_____
_____
_____

SAMPLE JOB DESCRIPTION OF A SALES PERSON

Supervisor: President/Vice President of Sales and Marketing

The primary role of the salesperson is to coordinate sales services in an assigned territory and provide technical marketing assistance as requested. Work involves calling on assigned accounts in a designated territory. The salesperson will decimate company materials, information, and data, maintain electronic and paper filing systems, and maintain a home office. The salesperson will act as a sales liaison with accounting, human resources, manufacturing, plant operations, purchasing, and all involved departments.

Requirements:

- College or relevant technical training. Experience in sales and/or marketing preferred.
- Exceptional interpersonal, listening, organizational, and critical thinking skills.
- Ability to work with an interdisciplinary team of professionals including technical staff, business and accounting staff, and sales team professionals.
- Ability to speak effectively to individuals and /or groups of varying sizes.
- Valid driver's license and a good driving record.
- Availability to travel.
- Availability to work occasional weekends.
- Availability to attend events on a regional, national, or international level.

- Attendance at annual corporate staff meetings and trainings.
- Ability to communicate in a skillful manner while simultaneously building credibility and rapport.

Professional appearance.

- Ability to manage time and meet deadlines since work is generally critical, confidential, and deadline driven.
- Be a highly organized, reliable, responsible, professional, and punctual individual.
- Work on complex assignments that are confidential in nature. Must exercise considerable judgment and initiative to resolve problems and make recommendations.
- Strong computer skills with editing abilities and familiarity with MS Office including Excel, PowerPoint, Word, and Outlook.

Duties:

- Assist with the day-to-day sales job functions for the sales department.
- Answer and return phone calls, maintain files, schedule meetings, maintain calendars, process mail, and handle routine correspondence.
- Track weekly, bi-weekly and monthly reports.
- Assist with monitoring sales contests.
- Track, compile, and maintain all sales department required forms.

- Maintain home office supplies as required by the sales department.
- Coordinate travel itineraries or business related trips, including air travel, lodging, conference rooms, food, agendas, presentation materials, etc.
- Record detailed and accurate minutes of all sales meetings.
- Provide customer service to incoming callers, screen and direct to appropriate staff, answer questions, resolve needs, etc.
- Assist Vice President of Sales in preparation for National Sales Meetings. Develop PowerPoint presentations, assembles notebooks, and assist in all aspects of event preparation.
- Prepare reports and spreadsheets as needed.
- Maintain contact database.
- Coordinate the process of marketing documents from start to finish.
- Support marketing logistics of trade shows, events and annual meeting.
- Maintain marketing inventory system and make replacement recommendations.
- Participate in new sales staff orientation on all sales processes, forms, electronic media, etc. as assigned
- Provide updates for company website as new information is identified.
- Assist other Executive Team Members on projects as assigned.
- Other duties as assigned.

I have read the above and agree to provide these services as part of my position.

Employee Signature
Date:

Supervisor Signature
Date:

23349385R00078

Made in the USA
Columbia, SC
07 August 2018